LIGHTEN the LOAD

This frank, funny, and wise book offers practical guidance.
- Comforting chapters about how to comfort others
- The relief of knowing how you have power at your own time of death
- Easy steps for making your own wishes known
- Simple guidance for standing by a sick relative, or a grieving co-worker
- Exercises for unlocking mindsets and relieving fears
- Handy lists for organizing your affairs

— Christiane Schlumberger, Editor

Lightening my load changed my life. By getting my <u>own</u> papers in order, "not leaving a mess for others," I grew personally and professionally. I learned to refuse a position of authority, to gain people's trust by sitting lower than the patient or the troubled family, even if that meant grabbing a stool or kneeling on the floor. A quick trick to keep me honest, all by the height of my seat! Sensible things!

— Cathy Bautista, R.N.

Frozen with fear, I avoided my pal dying of a brain tumor. So I read this amazingly simple book and did the homework. It was <u>work</u>, took me weeks, but I was desperate.

Afterwards, I called my sick friend and said things I'd never have said before. That wonderful conversation meant so much to her, and was so easy!!

Being my mom's ally when she was dying was only possible after lightening my own load. I asked if we could stop giving her meds except for comfort, stop insisting she get her hair done, or even eat. My family and her nurses were relieved by the candor and simplicity.

Side benefit: now all <u>my</u> affairs are in order. I feel great!

— Marian Wilke, Corporate Manager

LIGHTEN the LOAD enhanced my patience, sensitivity, and understanding with people. Braving the "homework assignments" armed me for later managing my own cancer treatments valiantly. Now I keep this handy reference guide by my desk, next to the dictionary and the phone book.

— Janet Jacobs, Hospice Volunteer, recipient of Ojai's Outstanding Volunteer of the Year Award, 2012

Salguero calls it like it is, offers straight talk to people who need to hear it straight. This is a very comforting approach to complex and difficult situations in our lives.

— June Behar, Editor

There are many people searching for how to manage the last decade of life. The solution is in lightening the load.

— Charys Saylor, Social Worker, Supervisor, Children's Protective Services

As a notary, I see many people taking care of business – with Health Directives and Powers of Attorney. They are getting necessary paperwork done in timely fashion. I recommend that . . . and reading Salguero's book!

— Dale Hanson, Realtor

LIGHTEN the LOAD shares insights gleaned from personal experiences - a wealth of handy tips. Everything Salguero wrote has worked for me. Her early printout of this handbook was a treasure I kept for years in a bottom drawer in my bedroom to refer to as each new family crisis arose. Now it is available to everyone!

— Debbie Hill, Director of Volunteers, Ventura County Medical Center

LIGHTEN the LOAD

*Tips & Tools to Ease
Aging, Dying, Grieving*

Susan Salguero

Library of Congress Cataloging-in-Publication Data

Salguero, Susan
LIGHTEN the LOAD : Tips & Tools to Ease Aging, Dying, Grieving

1. Aging 2. Grieving 3. Caregiving 4. End of life issues
5. Grief counseling 6. Dying 7. Hospice 8. Advance directives
9. Self help 10. Funeral plans

Book design by Nancy Sandstrom
Permission to use cover photo by Coons Family

Published by
StarBright Books
P.O. Box 915, Ojai, CA 93024

Acknowledgements

To Marlene Spencer: this book is the result of her nurturing and wisdom, her vision and years of hard work to create and sustain our model community volunteer agency, providing deep human resources to everyone in our community — with a minimal financial budget and maximum of human riches.

In honor of the noblest of volunteers:
Don "Cooner" Coons
Bill Weaverling
Vera Mazurek
Toetie Hoganboom
Ruthie Marks
Ken Dunn
Janet Jacobs

In memory of Janet "Jazzbo" Shoemaker

Offered with gratitude to its wise and generous editors, Christiane Schlumberger and June Behar, and to Shed Behar for his support.

Also by SUSAN SALGUERO

The GACHÍ: My Gypsy Flamenco Quest (2009)

Table of Contents

Preface

Most 'healthy aging' books focus on diet and exercise—a losing battle because, try as we will, the body IS wearing out anyway.

Why not pick a WINNING battle? All the rest of our vast reaches of health—the social and emotional and cultural and intellectual health of the aging person—the gradual improvement, even redemption, of the aging person!

This book does not dwell on our aging body. Nor does it pretend to address the spiritual mysteries, the grandest and most private part of each of us.

Instead, it offers tips toward attaining social and emotional health as we proceed through the second half of our lifetime. We can be living and growing and improving until our very last breath. Let us nurture this psycho-social health with passion and adventure, humor and hope.

Introduction

In my first training as a hospice volunteer, I was taught the classic Kubler-Ross formula, that, when given a terminal diagnosis, people consecutively deny it, get angry, bargain against it, and many finally accept it. They come to a place of peace.

And I thought, "HEY! I want some of that!! How about, in my forties, I admit to death and I go through those phases quickly to acceptance, and then live the next half of my life at peace!!" I wanted to be at peace while I was living my life, not just at the end of it!! And I want that for you, the reader, too.

But there's a challenge ... those difficult decisions ... those end-of-life decisions ... To attain that peace now, they need to be made now, NOT at the end of life.

Oh, you don't want to think about that now? You don't want to think about possibly, maybe, one day, perhaps ... dying? About when and how you choose to die? About where you choose to be buried? Okay then, just allow things to take their course, and let the high-tech healthcare professionals maintain your old/sick/dying body as long as they possibly can, regardless of the degree of suffering for you or your family or your finances or our groaning insurance systems.

Some men say, "When I get like that, just take me out and shoot me." I guess they want their wife or daughter to spend the rest of her life in prison.

Or maybe you say, "Just let me go peacefully when it's my time"...? No one can obey you unless you put that on paper!

How? Here's just the book for you.

And here's how to use it: Read only ONE CHAPTER per WEEK. Mull it over during that week, discuss it with someone you feel safe with—that is, someone you can be completely honest with. That might be your spouse, your daughter, your next door neighbor, your golf buddy, your best friend, or someone else who is reading this book, too.

Then do your homework at the end of the chapter. Each assignment is a "home-cleaning" assignment, to give you a fresh bird's-eye view of your life, a self-therapy assignment which will help you clear out unresolved issues, the unnecessary blocks which can cause useless worry.

Mind you, this is very hard work.

And very, very rewarding.

Susan Salguero

LIGHTEN the LOAD

Tips & Tools to Ease Aging, Dying, Grieving

Chapter 1

ELDER CARE
"No Free Lunch!"

"Something has got to be done!!" they scream at me over the phone.

My desk is cluttered with referrals from concerned citizens who insist that:

"That old person should not be living alone any longer!"

"The place is trashy; her clothes are filthy."

"He wanders into my house to stay cool."

"It's a fire hazard, and I live next door!"

"I feel so sorry for her; she looks like she's in pain."

I always wind up our discussion saying, "That is going to be you and me, soon enough, if we do not take care of business NOW."

Who takes care of our old people—the ones who don't take care of themselves? Their neighbors are burned out. The family is scattered all over the planet and basically unavailable, and others really are doing the best they can.

A social-service non-profit community agency like a senior center or van transport program can help. A good neighbor could visit folks and assess their situation; send them a meal or an insurance consultant or a notary; take them to the doctor, talk to their doctor; deliver their groceries or medicine; call their kinfolk; try to cajole them into a bath; invite them for a day of fun at the local day care center for frail elderly; or just visit and sympathize and suggest, maybe get them in the van to the senior center for lunch. But they cannot do everything. They can lead the horse to water, but have no authority to make him drink.

And here is the news flash: NO ONE—not our charitable agency, nor well-meaning neighbors, nor kind police officers, nor the county government—nobody can take away that dirty old person's constitutional right to be dirty, to be at risk of dehydration or malnutrition and subsequently falling in his/her own home and breaking ancient bones. He has lived there 35 years and refuses to leave his home now. Until he is in a life-threatening situation, judged by very narrow legal definitions—a situation more appalling than I can describe here—nobody can take away his freedom.

Sometimes our American Constitutional rights, bless them, get in the way of our well-being. If we lose a marble or two, nobody has the power to protect us. That is why we need to get our affairs in order SOONER rather than later, while we still have our own power to protect our future selves.

Do you want someone to "put you where YOU belong"? Do you, too, plan to live out your days at risk in your own home? I beg of you to take care of things now, before you reach a state that brings worry to your good neighbors.

How? Read this book, take it to heart, make some good choices of your own, and you are off to a great start.

DEAR ELDERS

Here is a song I sing daily. Not a popular song, but right on pitch. If you are an elderly person living at home alone and needing companionship, there are MANY in your situation in this country, as you quickly become the majority age group! The best remedies are to get involved at the senior center or at the day care center for frail adults, where you can nurture new friendships; and also to learn to enjoy your quiet hours alone at home.

A good friend or neighbor is invaluable—but expecting more than three hours of their time per week to fill your needs is abuse of a good friend or neighbor. If you want personal attention at home, you must pay for it: $15 per hour minimum. If you want a live-in companion, you must pay for that, too: free room and board, plus salary. Few would leave the comfort of their own home, the economic security of a regular income, to spend time in your cluttered home for free. Of course, if you would be willing to leave your home and share another person's home, then you could more easily solve your need for companionship. If you are unwilling to do that, it is proof you are asking for more than mere company; you are asking for something that you must pay for.

Remember that people asking $15 per hour are not trying to steal your money; they are honest wage-earners trying to keep body and soul together. Six dollars might hire a teenager, and some are excellent employees. If you need more experience than that, you pay more than that. How much? I am asked. In my area recently, a good cook/competent housekeeper/gentle elder companion was paid a minimum of $150 for a 24-hour day.

Perhaps you say all you need are some occasional errands and personal assistance and housekeeping. But in effect, you are asking for a maid and a butler. If you could not afford that thirty years ago, the chances are you cannot afford it now.

Granted, it is very disappointing that you have spent a lifetime socking away a nice stash for "old age," a stash that is threatened with total extinction by a few months of hired help. This same economic crisis is hitting our middle-aged and young families just as hard as it is hitting you. If you cannot afford to hire someone to keep you in your house, those of the next generation may not be able to afford a house at all.

NO FREE LUNCH

There is a way for each and every one of us to be cared for when we become elderly. The greatest dilemma of elder care is when the elder in question is ABLE BUT UNWILLING to pay for his care. Or else, unable to pay for it but also unwilling to receive governmental assistance. (He remembers that the forerunner of the nursing home was called a "poor house" and he refuses to "take charity.")

So his solution is to lean on anyone nearby (neighbors, family, friends, church) to do for him so he will not have to face the fact that he cannot do for himself. Elderly people often ask me to refer someone who needs a place to live for free. Some appropriate companion. With rent and grocery bills so high these days, it seems like you have a lot to offer some appropriate companion. You are right.

However, perhaps your criteria for "appropriate companion" are too exacting. You ask for "another lady like me." Another lady like you probably has your same needs and her own big house, and maybe she does not feel like driving you to church or playing cribbage with you, or getting out a fresh roll of toilet paper for you in the middle of the night. Your offer of "free room and board" sounds fishy because it is fishy. You need to look at all the silent strings you attach to your offer, all the tiny expectations, the constant social demands, that you will be wanting to exact of your companion.

People who really need your hospitality—homeless families, mentally ill, addicts, immigrants who do not speak English, runaway teenagers who are fed up with parents' rules (or abuse) in their own homes—do not fit your criteria of "appropriate companion."

Frankly, "there is no free lunch," not even when you are elderly. When you can accept the fact that you have lost just a tiny bit more of your independence than you are willing to admit aloud, then you can look honestly at what you are hiring and its actual dollar value. You would see that you are asking others to give what you might never have given. You have enjoyed the independence from family and segregation from younger people, which your generation so proudly created. Now you must pay the price.

So pay it fairly, and enjoy good help. Or, share the cost of care with others who need care too, in a retirement home. Or take that generous offer from your kinfolk across town or across the country, and move into their back room or granny flat, which they so loyally offer you. Then pay for that too!

HOMEWORK-1: Visit a "retirement home" or "assisted living facility" for a half hour. Take garden flowers and chat with a resident. (Ask a staff person if there is one who never has visitors and would appreciate one.) Then ask for a price list, and mentally figure what the residents are paying for—safety, comfort, clean linens, assistance when needed, three square meals, etc —and compare this with hotel prices.

ON TAMING YOUR ELDERS

Every week another exhausted, frustrated, loyal family member drops into my office. This is what these caregivers of the family elders need to hear:

While you look after aging Great Grandma, keep accurate records of time and money spent, then bill her estate.

Yes, of course she is incensed at this concept. During her childhood, extended families all lived together or nearby. The care of her grandmother was provided by many hands in the home (and that grandmother died at age 53, not 93). So now, Great Grandma expects you to do the same for her. For decades.

But nowadays you have only one pair of hands and they are committed elsewhere. Maybe you are maintaining a second marriage and household of your own, and the energy you spend on her is causing serious marriage erosion. Or perhaps you cannot afford the luxury of being kept in your home by your working husband. Great Grandma doesn't see that the time you spend on her is costing you big dollars in lost salary. Really, she hails from a different era, and in her deep need, she might never understand. So do not make promises you cannot keep.

Yes, there is great merit in family loyalty and gently harboring our elderly. But when Grandma saps your marrow in daily care, yet hoards her assets so her favorite nephew can inherit them, this injustice makes me cranky. And I have been cranky a LOT lately. I gnash my teeth when the only daughter is depleted after years of serving the folks day and night, yet when they die, the estate will be divided equally among three children.

There is a generation of elders who take pride in leaving an inheritance to relatives, and so they refuse to spend any of it on their own care. Usually those relatives do not need Great Grandma's money as badly as she does. She is living decades longer than she ever thought she would. All those years she was saving for "that rainy day." If she has outlived her own energy and competence, IT IS RAINING.

So, I beg her to spend her money on the help she needs, or else to please sponge off the very relatives who will inherit her riches. If not, I strongly encourage you designated family caregivers to bill the estate for the care and housing you have provided your elder. No, not $200 a month! Think $2,000 a month, minimum. It is good honest money, and you EARNED it!

A HOUSEKEEPER IS NOT A THERAPIST

Now that we are living a century, as we find ourselves looking after our loved ones in their very last years, we need help in the home. While counseling seniors to hire good assistance because they are confined, or because their elder is confined, many time I find myself teaching good employer etiquette—too late, because the cow is already out of the barn. The employee is taking advantage because you became her buddy, or her benefactor, or her inferior, taking orders from her—because of opening your private life and vulnerability to her, because of letting her private life merge into yours.

Do not make your housekeeper your therapist. You do not pay her enough. And do not become your housekeeper's therapist. She does not pay you at all.

If you are lonely, please go into chat rooms on the Internet, get a pen pal, or join a local support group, or a hobby club, such as stamp collectors or gardeners. Go out and volunteer, spending time with others. But do not make your employee your bosom buddy.

Do not fool yourself. Whoever comes to your house for money is not your best friend. You are operating with her under a business contract. It should be on paper, even if informally between the two of you, so that you can both refer to it later if there are misunderstandings, unmet expectations, or a feeling of being exploited or cheated.

Business is business. And whenever money is involved—IT IS BUSINESS. Mix business with pleasure, pleasure with therapy, or money with love—and sooner or later you will regret it.

This is called "keeping good boundaries," and it comes from the bad ol' days when people believed that "familiarity breeds contempt." But with household employees—that is the truth!

You might like and respect your employee—that is no grounds to tell her your marital problems. You must remember she comes to you because you pay her, and you must give her no more obligation than what she applied for. It is no more appropriate to make your employee your intimate confessor, than to make her your intimate sexual partner.

You hoped she would come iron and cook, or take care of your old dad while you iron and cook. But because you invited all the information about her tumultuous life, you find yourself harboring her from her abusive boyfriend, or from arrest, or from her financial crisis due to her addictions, or listening for hours on end about her trials raising her teenagers.

The less you both know about each other, the easier it is to stick to business. You'll be more inclined to give her a raise because she is finishing her tasks, and she in turn will do the job for you instead of sitting around over a cup of coffee while you confess and whine.

You pay, you say. She labors, then leaves. That is how it works.

> *HOMEWORK-2: Find a friend who hires help in the home or yard, and, like a journalist, ask questions about the employee, and LISTEN:*
> 1) *Is s/he a good worker?*
> 2) *Is s/he a good friend?*
> 3) *Is there a written agreement or task list of what's expected?*
> 4) *Is s/he paid well and is the boss getting his/ her money's worth?*

CAREGIVERS ANONYMOUS

We need Caregivers Anonymous like we have Alcoholics Anonymous. Suppose you marry a fine partner who will care for you the rest of your marriage. Then one day the brain of that spouse is damaged by a stroke or Alzheimer's or by hardening of the arteries. Due to the partner's slowly looming dementia, your life has become a silent scream; you are in a state of constant vigil and your days are 36 hours long.

Strangely, you do not ask for help. Your tendency is to hide the problem, like the enabling spouse of an alcoholic hides the drinking— you pretend that your life together has not become impossible. The bond of your marriage has become bondage. You think there is something wrong with you if you cannot manage it all by yourself. Any minor sense of ineptitude you once had has mushroomed into major inadequacy. You loathe yourself, work overtime to over-compensate, then resent all the work. And you still love your sweetie.

Daily life becomes a nightmare, and the sorrow is so deep and interminable that you do not know where to turn. So the tendency is to stay home and isolate and harbor that very needy spouse, by yourself. Soon home becomes your prison, and the dementia becomes the disability of two people. The care-giving spouse lives in shackles. These shackles of resentment, embarrassment, exhaustion, and grief slowly lead to ulcers, heart attack, depression. One husband of an Alzheimer's patient lamented: "This is the disease that kills two people."

Do you realize there is a way out? You can remain loyal to your beloved, yet get your own life back. You can get guidance, visit all your options, and find good help. It is available.

You also need grief counseling, so that you can grieve as you watch your sweetheart die ever so slowly before your eyes. Once you come out of "denial" and acknowledge, "accept" that you have lost the person you married, and gained a difficult patient instead, you will be on the way to recovery.

If your disabled person were to spend the day at your local adult day care center, you might visit and find a puppy on his lap, or find her dancing to oldies-but-goodies, or eating a nutritious lunch among friends—other disabled people who do not judge or rush. You might see teasing, people exercising on the lawn, or arranging flowers, or making soup, or just sitting enjoying each others' company.

There are adult day care centers for people with frailties — frail legs, frail eyes, or frail memories. People who have become isolated because of their inability to manage a simple social life of their own, come here to find one managed for them.

But, you protest, a day care center will not work for you and the person you care for? Come to a gathering of others in your same boat. Come to a caregivers' support group and learn all the other options for getting help. Learn you are not alone; learn that we ALL become ogres when our exhaustion and sorrow catch up with us. You will leave your group laughing, and go home comforted, re-energized to be that loving caregiver you really are.

MARGARET AND FRANK

We were all laughing in our caregivers' support group, our haven, when Margaret tattled on Frank. Almost five feet tall, Margaret had sharp black eyes, an easy giggle, and she grew the best bell peppers in her tract-house backyard. Neither Margaret nor Frank had any siblings, nor children, so when they married, besides lovers they became each other's brother and sister, and child. When he developed Alzheimer's, she just continued to care for him like her child, even when, in his confusion, he got a little rough.

One evening Frank couldn't understand that she wanted him to sit at the kitchen table for dinner like they had for 55 years. So he shoved her away, and being a wiry little old guy, he sent Margaret flying across the kitchen landing on her butt against the sink cabinet. She wasn't badly hurt and took it in her stride, but the next day he elbowed her with a sly grin.

"Boy, last night I sure sent that old woman flying across the room, didn't I?" he boasted. She agreed through her tears and laughter, not even trying to tell him it was her.

By this time Margaret had caught the knack of finding the mirth in the ways of cruel fate. One time she sat down next to him, put her arm around his shoulder, and said, "I love you; would you give me a kiss?"

He kissed her on the lips, then she asked, "Shall we tell your wife?" He stiffened, glared, and nearly smacked her, then wouldn't speak for hours. Until he forgot the incident. She chuckled over it for a long time, and so did we all, every time I re-told her stories in the support groups.

I sent a hospice volunteer to sit with Frank occasionally so Margaret could go do errands freely. He was watching TV, his rocker placed in front of it in the middle of the room, so the volunteer made herself comfortable on the sofa. Frank got up and began circling the rocker. He walked around it and around it, then changed directions and continued pacing circles around the rocker the other way, while the volunteer watched. After continuous circling and reversals, he stopped suddenly and plopped down beside the volunteer.

"OK, I'm tired. You take over for a while," he said.

LIE-CHEAT-AND-STEAL

Going nuts caring for a loved one with dementia? Someone who is more than forgetful, who also has lost cognitive ability? Caring for someone whose good brain has been damaged by an accident or stroke or progressive illness? Someone who no longer can take care of her/himself?

Are you discovering that his/her independent life is a shambles? You call to remind her, you leave notes taped to the kitchen cupboard, but nothing works? You explain to him that he no longer has a license, but he takes the car for a drive anyway? She fills her pantry with nothing but Ajax, yams and Bisquick? You tell her about her dentist appointment next month, so she has already packed her overnight case to get ready? You find her unbathed and smelly, and discover she now fears the shower? He/she can no longer manage the thermostat, or the tangled Venetian blinds? Looking for the toilet, she winds up squatting on the kitchen wastebasket, or he sprays the corner of the living room? S/he is awake most of the night, wandering the house? Or you leave him comfortably at home but then you return from an errand to find him inexplicably gone (and police find him wandering the streets in pajamas)?

The fact is that this person can no longer be trusted. You cannot depend on this person, be protected by this person, be advised by this person. It is a whole new sad world here. A world where roles are reversed and now YOU are the grown-up; YOU are the spouse in charge.

Your dementia patient cannot decipher your words, so slowly you need to learn to omit most information, to say only the simple and tolerable. You don't advertise appointments or plans ahead of time. It helps to be specific, addressing only the present moment, with only one single request. Nothing complex such as explaining you are going to go pick up the kids at school, then go to soccer practice and get to the dentist appointment, then have dinner at the Sizzler. Instead you only say, "Let's put on your coat, here's your sleeve."

Your dementia patient cannot remember or figure out what to do or not do, so you remove temptations and the confusing items they used to use easily, but now pose some danger. You're forced to cut the plugs off the dangerous power tools, to hide all the car keys, or remove the distributor cap. Or maybe you park the car out of sight and tell him it is in the shop for repairs.

You fudge so he can win at cards, or backgammon, you sneak your trout on the end of his line, or you slip the meds he refuses to take in his applesauce or his coffee. To get her to the doctor you say, "Come with me while I go to the doctor. Hold my hand. Here's the scale, lets weigh both of us."

YOUR mind is still good, so you have to use it to cover for his/her mind that isn't. Contrary to your old sense of integrity, you have to be diplomatic in a whole new way. We have nicknamed this "**lying-cheating-and-stealing**." Out of compassion for the person whose brain no longer provides the necessary information to care for himself, "**lying-cheating-and-stealing**" simplifies life, reduces distress.

If you continue to honor your brain-damaged spouse or parent with your former respect by giving choices, asking opinions, allowing privacy, then actually you are the one with the problem. It is YOUR problem because only you know that you cannot reason with and un-reason-<u>able</u> person.

But, you object, you cannot bring yourself to be dishonest? First you must grieve. The person you once depended upon has left. By grieving, you progress from denying the dementia to admitting the dementia and acting accordingly. You must learn to not believe him, not trust him, not argue with him, not reason with him, and not persuade him.

Does Dad in his senility insist on cashing his income check and carrying all that money in his wallet, which he is constantly misplacing? You contrive to remove the money and replace it with a pad of one dollar bills sandwiched between two twenties. That keeps his money safe, keeps peace in the house and keeps you sane.

Contrary to your upbringing or your scruples, the antidote for tragic dementia in the family is to **lie-cheat-and-steal**.

INDEX OF VITAL INFO

Most of us have a "person," the one we trust the most with our personal issues, our household, etc., the one who has a key to our house: a spouse, partner, relative, best friend or neighbor. But it is one thing to trust them, and quite another to actually give them the tools to help us when we are temporarily out of commission. We've all laughed at stories of the husband who, when mom was hospitalized with appendicitis, fumbled running the household, not knowing when the school bus came, or where to get the puppy's shot.

Suppose you were called away from home for an extended period—months even. Could you quickly turn over your home and affairs to someone to manage while you are gone? Or, what if you become impaired, seriously ill, hospitalized, or simply grew old and bewildered? Or died unexpectedly, leaving your household in major chaos?

The best tool you could give your helper would be an index of all your vital information and/or its whereabouts, all listed on one handy worksheet. My suggestion, as I did for my mother and my disabled son: get permission and make a list of Vital Info for everyone you might have some responsibility for.

AN INDEX OF VITAL INFO — SUGGESTED ITEMS:

- My Name/Address/P.O. Box/Phones/E-mail
- Driver's License#/SS#/DOB
- Autos: license#, model and year, VIN, where pink slip is filed, insurance co. and policy #, locations of all keys, service records
- Dependents: names, DOB, SSN#, nicknames, teachers, social workers, MDs, alternate caretakers, etc.
- Pets: name, breed, color, age, food and feeding times, medicine, toilet regimes, alternate caretakers, commands understood, veterinarians, habits and fears, medical/shot history
- Property maintenance: names, phone #, landlord, plumber, gardener
- MDs: name, specialty, phone #, address, appointment frequency, prescribed medications, dosages, pharmacy phone #
- Broker, Investor, Account #
- Income sources: when, where, how paid
- Banking: bank, account type, account #. Safe deposit box – location of key
- Clubs/Associations: contact names and phone #
- Monthly bills (rent, utilities, gym, mortgage, car payment, credit cards, phones, internet, cable TV) account # or location of old bills

- Debts owed to me and by me
- Insurances: where policies filed, claim #, company name, phone #
- Wills/trusts/power of attorney: where filed, attorney's name and phone #
- Legal documents – where to find certificates: (birth/baptism/death/ guardianship/conservatorship/marriage/divorce/adoption)
- Funeral preferences, mortuary address, phone #
- List of all acquaintances to be notified at your death, communities which should have your obituary
- Valuables: history, value, where stashed, alternate guardian, how to repair and/or sell them.
- Computer codes, e-addresses, pin codes, location of back-up drives, etc.

> *HOMEWORK-4: Make your own Index of Vital Info, with copy for a trusted person. (And insist upon an Index of each person and pet for whom YOU are responsible.)*

Chapter 2

NURSING HOMES
"Those Places"

We abhor nursing homes because they seem to threaten us with death. But let's put the blame where it really belongs.

Nursing homes in America have a terribly bad rap. But their alternatives are so much worse. Your skin stuck to a sidewalk in Calcutta. Dying out on the ice in Alaska. Your family doing your laundry and packing meals from home, in southern Spain. Our nursing homes are cushy, and yet we despise them.

"Don't you ever put me in one of 'those places'," we exhort our families. And yet we live so long that we have exhausted all other hands besides the paid ones—the four hands it takes to heave us onto the toilet in the nursing home.

Actually, we object to being dependent upon the care of others, to becoming impaired, helpless, blithering, while still alive. Perhaps we are not as scared of death as of not dying quickly, in tidy fashion. So we make the nursing home the scapegoat, transferring onto it the horror we feel about our own loss of control. We abhor it unjustly, like the boats blaming the harbor for the storm. We should not be blaming nursing homes for our misery. We should blame our misery for nursing homes. You tell me which hotel provides a clean bed daily, three squares, a personal attendant to bathe and dress you, literally wipe your bottom for you, deliver clean laundry to your closet, and invite you with a friendly smile to socialize with your neighbors in the lounge—all for only $100 or $200 a day!

If you want more than that, why are you not paying more? And if you prefer to stay home where it is free, think again. Staying home with that kind of service will cost you double the cost of the nursing home—while you are also still paying for the mortgage, the utilities, the toilet paper, and meat and potatoes (pureed), on top of that.

How to avoid residence in a nursing home? Die before you need it. I figure, if I have all my 'affairs in order,' keeping them updated, then when they put me in that nursing home, I will be ready. With good luck, a wonderful nurse's aide (I have seen plenty) will keep me clean and powdered, smooched and tucked in, ready to go. I will see the handwriting on that dreary wall—that it's time to die—and once I get over my rage about out-living myself and stop punishing the help by pooping on their clean sheets, once I've had enough of being handled, then fast as you can snap your fingers, I'll be out of there—dead as a doornail, free as a bird, high as a kite.

I often hear someone groan, "Oh, I can't put Mom in that place. She'd die if I put her in there."

And all I can think to say is, "Good for her."

My own intention is to spend no more than a few days or weeks in a nursing home.

I lived in a monastery in India for three years. I went there of my own accord. I needed to retreat from the world, to leave worldly drives and distractions behind, to have my room and board provided, in utter simplicity, so that I could focus fully on my spiritual life. No social life, no power over others, no name, no mirror to comb my hair—the monastery was a vacation from my desires and fears—a chance to accelerate my riddance of self-interest. Bathroom sounds and smells were shared with the community. There was no entertainment but prayer and devotional sing-alongs. A retreat, it was a halfway house between my former worldly life and the spiritual grace I sought thirstily. I became anonymous even to myself, and the purity of my soul, my innate joy, the utter proximity of the divine, became my daily life, my total immersion. All that beauty thanks to the austerity of the monastery.

When I returned to this life in Ojai, I was super-charged with love. The only job I could find was that of activities director in a nursing home. And all my stored love was showered on the patients and staff of that nursing home. I noticed that the old, wrinkled, wheelchair-bound inhabitants were also on retreat in a kind of monastery. Personal possessions and privacy left behind, like mine. No longer in power over their world, fed and kept safe while they too did nothing but contemplate.

I laughed at them when they would act out their old worldly resentments and gripes and rivalries. I thrilled to see them learn humility, patience, tolerance, forgiveness and dispassion. I hugged them, teased them, raced with them in wheelchairs, played games and sang songs with them while they waited for their turn to die. But I never pitied them. The nursing home was their monastery, their halfway house on their journey to heaven. They too were in an accelerated program to get Home, and all I could do was cheer them on, and wish them a speedy journey.

You know, folks, if the monastery and the nursing home were glamorous and catered to our selfish whims—we would never get anywhere.

But, you say, the old people did not choose to go there. Perhaps not, but they stay until they are ready to get out. Some people can die quickly from their house, but those of us too attached to our pride, our anger, our desire to control others, our sensuous pleasures, our favorite complaints, our possessions, all the things of this material world— we need time to wean ourselves. We need that extra boost which the austerity of the monastery or the nursing home can give us, in order to lift off.

STRATEGIES

Most folks valiantly resist using nursing homes for their loved ones. Perhaps you do, too. You kept him home with you, caring for him yourself. You tried hiring help in the home. You moved him into a fine retirement home, but he needed more than 'assistance.' So again he is home, ruining your back, depriving you of sleep and your sense of humor. Exhausted to tears, numb, inept, and depressed, a caregiver gets cranky. Your children and your fellows in your caregivers' support group badger you about placing him before YOU are hospitalized. So finally you cave. You do it. You determine to place him in a nursing home. Feeling like a traitor for 'abandoning' him, you are tormented by guilt.

Most nursing homes are not as bad as our prejudice. Let them be. They have improved over the years, and some can be a perfect fit for your family member. Allow them to be the necessary tool when your beloved outlives his own ability of self-care.

When Pops is too old and frail to keep his home clean, repaired, and watered; when he cannot feed himself out of his own fridge; when he cannot hear the phone or he babbles; when he no longer aims at the toilet; when he dehydrates; when he jeopardizes his life with his own medications; when he falls and cannot get up—then HIS HOME HAS BECOME OBSOLETE. He needs help to manage in it. If he cannot afford hired help, and he has worn you out, then he must move to share space and hired help with others.

YOU are placing him. But, all on his own, HE has outlived his ability to manage himself. Not yet willing to leave his worn-down bones, he must wait somewhere until he is willing. His nursing home is the waiting room in his train station. It is his responsibility (dementia or no) to get out of here when he has outlived his own usefulness to himself. When he does that is UP TO HIM and really is not your business, hence not your fault, hence not your guilt. Your job is to prepare yourself for launching out of here in timely fashion. Let him manage his own process.

When you browse, shopping for facilities, do not visualize yourself moving there. You are not—not as you are now. Try to see your patient clearly as he is now—not through the thick veneer of memories of his hard jobs and grand successes.

Right now, the man cannot pull up his pants.

See the facility through his current eyes and needs. Yes, home is always best—until it becomes overwhelming. A bland, clean, 'institutional' environment provides less sensory input, therefore less confusion, and less anxiety for him than a home environment. That which alarms you just might soothe him. Familiarity of home is a comfort until every item reminds him of the responsibilities he can no longer fulfill. This causes him anxiety even while he is protesting that home is where he must be. The heating system, a dripping faucet, paying bills, answering the phone, or opening the blinds, can cause great stress which might be relieved by becoming a 'guest' in a new place.

Urine odor is common in most nursing facilities in the morning when wet beds are first opened. Visiting hours are always in the afternoon, and by that time the smell should be gone. Instead of misjudging the staff, remember it's HIS incontinence, and be grateful to them.

Most men would rather have paid strangers cleaning up after them than feel the shame of kinfolk doing it. His relief at no longer being a burden to a family member can go undetected. Or perhaps he is relieved that his spouse or son or daughter can survive at home without him—the release he needs to move towards dying in peace.

"'Till death do us part"? Death used to be more sudden. Fact is, he is dying. He is no longer the man who sired you, no longer that man you married. His gradual demise requires the nursing home, whence he is slowly parting from you.

The nursing home might be provoking your sorrow caused by his infirmity and gradual decline. Yours is 'anticipatory grief' from admitting that you are losing him. Grief is healthy. Anticipatory grief is appropriate—as long as you do not scapegoat the nursing home. Consider it an advantage. Most families on this planet live in communities where no nursing homes exist, none at all!

Are you the villain when he keeps begging to 'go home' and you cannot comply? Often, families continue hearing that request even when they do take him home. I suspect 'home' to him is that time years ago when his mind still made sense of things, when he was wholly himself and in charge of his world. And sometimes 'home' is a metaphor for release from this body, for his conception of 'heaven.'

Even if he actually means the house he inhabited with you a week ago, you either can let that request feed your guilt, or you can remember that you did not steal from him his independence. His condition did that.

Were you in his place, would you want him to become a slave to your infirmities, or rather to carry on with his good life? Or else, ask yourself this: Would he keep you home, providing for your every need? Maybe you are not practicing the Golden Rule which says to do unto him that which he would do unto you were the tables turned. No, I am not asking you to be cruel and unfair to him. I am simply asking you to not be cruel and unfair to yourself.

The job of all caregivers is to care for two worthy people: the patient and the caregiver. The best way to take care of your husband is to take very good care of his wife, so that you can protect him as long as he lives. On the airplane, you put the oxygen mask over your own face first, before you put it over the face of your dependent companion. Same here. Keep yourself alive and well, so that you can be here for him. Do not kill yourself trying to do the job of many. Once his legs give out, it takes four hands to lift him into bed. You only have two.

So, your lover, the man of your dreams, your beloved husband, is in a nursing home. That is very, very sad. You must be much older, both of you, than when you first looked into each other's eyes. And that was the deal.

Or, he was your daddy, the one who taught you table manners, dancing and driving—this one who sadly cannot remember your name, cannot use a fork.

Grieve, and then be thankful for the nursing home aides who aid you in your care of him.

> *HOMEWORK-5: List retirement homes in your area, by their 'levels of care.' Which accept walking residents with dementia? Which accept wheelchair-bound residents? Visit a nursing home staff with a batch of cookies and thank them.*

SUPERVISING

From the folks in our support group, here are some great tips for you family caregivers who reluctantly might be placing a loved one in a nursing home. If you were a team supervisor, you would:

a) give simple instructions, make REASONABLE requests

b) not expect more than you pay for

c) praise, thank, give bonuses

d) chide your staff ONLY on crucial deviations from your requirements

Same with your nursing home staff:

1. They are your employees, an extension of your own care of him. You are not abandoning him. You visit frequently and randomly so they never know when you are coming—which keeps them honest.

2. You praise every little effort of the staff and reward them periodically with a box of candy or home baked cookies left

at the nurses' station with an appreciative note—which keeps them willing.

3. You are studiously careful to complain only once for every three times you praise—that's 1 to 3, folks—which keeps them receptive. You get into therapy or join your local caregivers' support group so that you do not attack the staff when it is YOU who are feeling guilty of negligence.

4. You NEVER require more than keeping him clean and pottied and fed and as comfortable as possible, considering his condition.

5. You cannot demand that they keep his possessions straight. You need to remember that he cannot afford a maid and a butler, and THEY are not his maid and butler. Family keepsakes and expensive gifts do not belong in the facility. Sweat suits and common colored lap-robes are better than a precious personal item with the demand that the staff keep track of it, which is not a 'reasonable' request.

6. This includes glasses, false teeth, and hearing aids. Things get misplaced in a public place, a group facility. Don't blame. Help with the search.

7. Have patience, and find your gratitude for these, our most underpaid and overworked employees in America. Determine to help them keep him spiffy, to lower your dress-code standards for him, to burden them no further with your criticism.

8. YOU can come by and carefully shave and cologne him. YOU can comb his hair the way you like it. YOU can pick out what you want to see him wearing. YOU can gussy him up for Sundays, and then take his good clothes home at the end of the day to launder, yourself. Maybe you could bring him home for family dinner.

9. You can take him out in the wheelchair for that daily walk, or play checkers, or listen to music with him, or bring his favorite ice cream sundae and favorite pet to sit with him.

10. Furniture choices are actually the worst drawback in a nursing home. There are only two: bed or wheelchair. A wheelchair is a vehicle, not comfortable enough for day-long sitting. We usually want to 'go home' either for the privacy and familiarity of our own bathroom, or for that chair which had become

the ONLY place where the bones do not hurt. His mangy old easy-chair is probably what he misses most. Why not make it a PRIORITY to get that chair by his bed in the nursing home?

11. You can make a list, in large print, of his proudest accomplishments during his lifetime and, with photo blowups, paper the wall over his bed with them, so that everybody there can know him, who he really is beneath that tired, worn-out frame. "Did you know that Hank was a cattle rancher, a motorcycle mechanic, owner of 23 dogs in his lifetime, an electrician, and a big strong outdoorsman who loved nature?!?" Norma's husband got better care from an interested staff after that great addition to his surroundings.

12. Every time you visit him, you can tell his roommate, or simply reminisce to him, about some grand event in his life, about each small accomplishment—in time, doing a thorough review of his life. Ask his other visitors to do the same—to praise, and tattle, and laugh together about his life—while he is still among you and able to hear it—even if he cannot contribute a word.

13. You can boost your own morale by visiting some other lonely soul there who has no family. Chat and bring treats or clippings. Brightening her day will brighten your otherwise dismal visit. Some nursing home residents can be very nurturing for you. Pick one.

14. You keep in mind that you could not do this job alone, but that you are still doing it with the assistance of 'your' staff. USE your nursing home well, don't abhor and avoid it! Find an adequate nursing home, or a very nearby one, knowing that a perfect one does not exist. Then continue to care for him there, providing the little niceties that you know he likes. Meanwhile you let the staff and nighttime workers and cooks do the brunt of the job which you cannot.

15 Sorrow is appropriate; blame is not. Grieve with him his loss of youth, health, capabilities and independence. Realize that these realities are the cause of his misery, not you and not 'your staff.' Admit that we NEED nursing homes. Bring smiles to 'your' employees, and take pride in your ongoing, imperfect care of your patient.

HOMEWORK-6: Write your own list of Social History facts (for wall of nursing home, or to assist whomever gives your eulogy), and add it to your Vital Info files.

SOCIAL HISTORY SUGGESTIONS:
Full name, other names, nicknames
Date/place of birth
Where you grew up
Parents' occupations
Education
Careers/jobs/occupations
Primary accomplishments
Primary interests/passions/hobbies
Pets/animal friends
Military service
Sports
Favorite vehicle
Favorite food
Health issues
Favorite authors/painters/musicians/sculptors/ books/poetry
Religious affiliation
Proudest moment/Most humbling moment
Greatest success/Strongest regret
Special treats
Favorite expressions of speech
Passions

LOVE STORY

My life as 'activities director' in a nursing home:

"SEE'S Chocolates!" the girls at the nurses' station exclaimed as I approached, handing them the box.

"They're just for you special girls. I carefully picked out all the calories." Old joke, but they all twittered. Grateful I didn't have their hard jobs, I paused behind one to rub her tired back.

"Lookout!" I warned. "Here comes Sadie Lee!" The aides

continued charting behind the counter. One snapped a binder closed and stood to re-shelve it, peering around the corner at Sadie Lee to make sure she was empty-handed.

"We had to take that cane away from her. She'd clobber anyone in her way." Sadie was barreling down the nursing home hallway in her wheelchair, pulling herself along the grab-rail, scooting with her one good foot. She coveted colors, sporting a dozen strands of colored beads around her neck, under her pure white braids. These were Bingo prizes that others—who played bingo only for the banter and fun company—had won in the community room. The beads made her proud, so Sadie gleaned all the prizes.

"Look at all her beads!"

"Yep," said the aide. "She's got 'um all. So now she goes from room to room stealing colored afghans donated by the local knitters." Sadie lurched by us around the corner and on the hunt.

"Nice flowers you've got here; must have been crafts day."

"Yes, our nice crafts lady hates crafts." That was me. So I had the residents do other handwork. They'd make soup—each one peeling potatoes or carrots, snapping beans—you sure got a lot of yakking over bean-snapping. Or wrap gifts, or arrange flowers. The locals would bring day-old flowers, recycling altar decorations or centerpieces, or funeral sprays, and I'd collect wide-mouth jars for easy arranging. The aide pointed to a bouquet above her on the countertop.

"This one's our favorite, from Viola." It looked a little scraggly—one tall gladiolus and a few geraniums and daisies. We all ogled it, grinning. Floating in the bottom of the jar, among the stems, was a set of dentures.

I crossed the hall to Daisy Porter, hulking over in her wheelchair. A persistent whimper rolled from her slack mouth. Her leather grimace could belong to Sitting Bull's mother-in-law, with jutting cheekbones, angular nose, toothless gums. Her jowls hung lower than her chin and swung like a rooster's wattle as she whimpered. So many skin awnings folded out over her eyelids that I had to squat down to lap level to gaze up under them into that swimming-pool blue.

"Hi, Daisy Porter." My voice was throaty with love.

Daisy Porter raised brows to lift the many lids and peer

out from under them to study the person crouched before her wheelchair.

"Who are you?" Daisy asked with a startled look, startlingly blue. She seemed to sort through a century of faces, trying to place this one.

"You don't know me, Daisy Porter. I only love you." My eyes stung, I loved so fiercely, gazing up into that mammoth old human face. Daisy picked at the yellow flowered smock on this young woman squatting before her, and stroked my hair with a big worn paw. Then folds dropped back over her eyes, and jowls jiggled as she whimpered again.

"What's the matter, Daisy Porter?" I dropped a friendly arm across the bone-lap, and patted the old boulder of a knee.

"I want to go to bed."

"Are you tired, Daisy Porter?"

"Yep," she complained with a voice that had talked since before telephones were invented. "Bakin' cakes all day long."

It was only ten o'clock in the morning. But at the age of 102, it was late—long past time to trundle off to rest. Built like a horse, Daisy had lived too long to remember how to die. She was born knowing how to cry and breathe and seek a nipple, how to make babies and nourish them, but Daisy somehow had lost that last knack of dying. Stuck in life, she whimpered her exhaustion. Tenderly, I laughed at her, nosing up into her jowls to smooch her.

"You've just got to wait."

"Been a-waitin' for that bus. It never comes."

"It will come, Daisy Porter," I affirmed. "Might as well wait with the rest of us in here."

I stood up and pushed Daisy's wheelchair into the dining room for 'sing-along,' where Ginger's piano music would lull her.

I did not believe in these inane 'activities' which I was paid to 'direct' for the nursing home residents. But then, I didn't believe in living over a hundred, either. I knew that as long as you dwelt in a body, you needed movement to keep the dwelling inhabitable; that if you were interested enough in life to complain, you were interested enough to require the company of others. Humans are social beings, and they ossify in isolation. I didn't care whether they DID activities, but I believed they needed EACH OTHER. Company could provoke a moment's merriment. My job was to help them find their own smiles, even at age 85 or 102. I loved my job. A nursing home is indeed a 'warehouse,' like a monastery is: providing basic body needs while you detach from your belongings, from your own power, from your self-importance; so that you can move on. Like my ashram life was, nursing home life is a halfway house between life and freedom—freedom from selfishness, from stuff we 'can't take with us,' either to die or to realize God, or both. My old folks were in training here, making ready to move on, and I had not a crumb of pity for them. I walked elated among them, and for them.

My beige Nikes skimmed miles around the polished corridors. My very first 'running shoes' felt like rubber compassion under my retired dancer's feet. I overtook another wheelchair, a self-propelled one, and asked,

"Where ya goin', Sadie Lee?" I asked. "The music's back that way."

"Ah'll get thar. Goin' clear around." Pretty as Mrs. Claus, Sadie Lee. Her two thick braids of curly hair, pure white as cotton, now dangled over the back of her chair.

"Well, come around for music. How pretty your braids are!" I exclaimed, fondling them.

"Yup. Muh daughter-in-law come and fixed 'um for me. Ah never cut muh har in muh whole life. You should have seen muh momma's har—black as coal and clear to the floor. Muh daddy made me promise Ah'd never cut mine neither."

"You come to the dining room so Ginger can see your hair."

"Yup," concurred Sadie as she grabbed the handrail to heave her chair another few yards down the hall.

I skirted the med-cart. "Hello, Nursie," I teased the stern R.N. who tapped pills into a tiny paper cup.

"Say, Smarts, get to work."

"Yes, ma'am, yes'um, as you say ma'am," I vowed, turning into the next room.

All 85 pounds of Hazel sat prim and hunchbacked, with set little jaw and asymmetrically placed eyes, ready for the day in the child's wheel chair, her tiny clean hands crossed on her lap, her laced shoes as white and proud as Sadie's hair.

"Come on, Hazel. My volunteer isn't coming today; I'm

counting on you to help me host the folks."

"Well, all right." Wrinkling her nose in distaste, Hazel conceded, "I'll do it for YOU."

"Thank you, Hazel. Has Harold's daughter been in yet?"

"No, I haven't seen her." Hazel was the local chamber of commerce: her memory intact, and her room just inside the front entrance. "Would you get out that clipping I want to give her, please?"

"Sure."

"It's in the pink candy box on my bedside table, just under the Bible. Put that chair back so Sadie Lee can't get past it. She takes anything she can reach. What a pest."

I retrieved the paper, replaced the flounced maple barricade and headed Hazel's wheelchair down the hall.

"I marked my place in my Bible; I want you to read that Psalm."

"Yes, before I go home tonight." Hazel would be sitting up in bed, a miniature princess with lop-sided face and pink crocheted bed jacket, writing letters or reading her Bible. For eleven years this had been her home, and the classiest home this poor Kentucky spinster ever knew. I'd sit on the foot of Hazel's bed, read, and chat about my son, Frankie. It was my reward after a day's work—for Hazel loved me. And Hazel talked about her Lord. Once Hazel confided, "I know the curtains will part and my Lord Jesus will hold out His hand. I'm ready to go any time." (A few years later those curtains of the Lord's would part to find Hazel sitting on the toilet.)

As I swept Hazel down the hall, I complained, "You know I'm still disappointed that you didn't come home with me for Christmas this year."

"It was raining," explained Hazel, "I could have caught my death of cold." She couldn't see me laughing at the irony as her chair joined the circle gathering around the piano.

I next wheeled in Mrs. Townsend. Instead of heading for the piano, I pulled up at a full-length mirror. Mrs. Townsend sat proud and coiffed, but she had been sick for two months and had lost all sense of time and place. So, at the mirror, I exhorted, "Just see how nice you look today, Mrs. Townsend."

That beautiful old woman with aquiline profile and

demeanor as elegant as an empress stared at the 90-year-old woman looking back from the mirror. Astonished at her own reflection, she leaned forward and exclaimed, "My land! Will you look at that!"

I remembered feeling that astonishment while studying a recent photo of my Frankie. He was fifteen, looking eleven, leaning against the orange fender of my bruised blue VW square-back. It took me a moment to notice the middle-aged woman standing next to my son, then to realize that it was his mother!

Ginger, glad Ginger, breezed in with her music books, her wide-eyed good humor and the humility of a monk. She greeted and gabbed, scuffed out the piano bench, chose a music book out of her stack, whipped up the old songs that Viola could harmonize, the hymns that pleased Hazel, the popular ditties of the Twenties that Ruth remembered best. Ginger's banter uplifted everyone, even the nurses who stopped in.

"Well, Mabel, here's your song. "Down in the Valley." It says it was first sung in 1910 by..."

I left them all with Ginger, while I visited the folks who stayed in bed.

Next morning, the dining room of the nursing home was silent. Fifteen people sat there, but no one was speaking. Sitting in wheelchairs, staring at bright knitted afghans in laps, three asleep with mouths ajar and dentures askew. I strode in, carrying the bingo bag, plopping it on the circled tables, my voice dispelling the silence.

"Well, THIS is a lively bunch! Whew! Rise and shine everybody! Do I need to go into a lil' song and dance routine here?" I greeted Mabel with a grin, a handshake, and finger to lips: "Shhhhh, don't talk. Don't wake up Harry here. Mustn't disturb his repose." This whimsy tickled Mabel, who had lost her speech. And Harry's eyes popped open.

"What's the matter, Harry," I chided, "the nurses keep you up all night?" He nodded. His eyes twinkled for a fraction of a moment as I carefully shook his left hand, the good one.

"Good morning, sir." His eyes followed me around the room.

"Mary, good morning. Did your daughter return?"

"Yes, a few days ago. Was I glad to see HER." Mary's feet and ankles were swollen fatter than her legs, bigger than her skin should stretch, but her hair was still brown and her mind wasn't worn. However, she would die before all the others.

"That's a relief, Mary. Would you mind sitting next to Mabel here, to help her with her bingo card?"

"Glad to."

"Thanks so much. That OK with you, Mabel?" Mabel nodded, pleased that SOMEbody asked HER opinion.

"Hazel, I'll put you between Harry and Maudie here, so you can kinda prompt them." I knew that Hazel wouldn't play bingo. No gambling was going to ruin her chances of getting into heaven, after earning it with 85 years of virgin chastity. She was too close to risk a mistake now.

"Viola P. Brown, good morning. Let me move you right up to the table here for bingo. Viola, you sure harmonized with Ginger yesterday. I bet you never sang the actual melody to any song in your life."

With a handshake and a loving gaze, I greeted every person in the room, seating them around the table, doling out enlarged bingo cards.

"Warm hands, Ethel! Mine are icy still. I can't let go of yours. Toast mine up here. Thank you. It is COLD up there on my hilltop! I sleep on a screened porch, and my breath makes clouds all night long, 'til snow falls! First time I ever owned an electric blanket."

"Well, you NEED it, dear," affirmed Mary with grandmotherly concern.

"Yes, but it is so beautiful up there. I just roll out of bed, grab my stocking cap, and I'm out walking before my eyes click open. And before anyone else is up, I'm on my hilltop, looking across the valley at the Topas. Got a sneak view of the new snow on them before the sun came up and drew the mist over them. DID YOU ALL KNOW THAT THERE IS SNOW ON THE BLUFFS TODAY? While it was raining on us, it was snowing on them.

"Are you all ready to play? I'll stay here near Ethel's warm hands." I remained standing so that I could move freely among them. My tokens clattered in their basket as I ran my fingers through them to toss them. "Put your chip on the free square.

Here's the first number. G, 46. Gee, four six. You've got it, Sadie. You, too, Mabel. Now there's to be 'no cheating unfairly.'"

That brought a smile to most of the aged faces. It was understood that they didn't care any more about the game than I did, nor for the trinkets they might win. Except for Sadie Lee. Like a magpie, she hoarded anything colorful. Long ropes of bright beads spilling into her lap, she had extra earrings clipped to the collar of her house dress. In fact, my green-plastic-handled paring knife, which I used when discussing and serving local fruit, was gone for two months, until I thought of its pretty apple-green handle and searched Sadie's bedside table.

"B, 4. Bee, four." I exchanged knowing looks with Hazel while inquiring, "Sadie, you aiming to win a little something today? ... 0, 75 ... Oh, seven five ... Look! Lulu's arrived. Our champ is here!"

Lulu grinned as her big swollen feet perambulated the chair into the room, proud that she won first place in my 'annual' wheelchair races, after refusing for two years to use a wheelchair. Lulu's medal, a paper plate and a doily with construction-paper heart, still hung over her bed. I thought of how Lulu welcomed my son, Frank, the first time he visited her room after school. I'd apologized to her that he'd changed channels on her TV.

"Well, of course he can watch what he wants on my TV, he's MY boy," declared Lulu with that unconditional love of all small beings an ancient person can muster.

"I, 21. I, two one. Well, now," I teased, "We agree you may play with us, Lulu, but can you keep from crying if you lose?"

"Mebe I'll find me another bingo game," laughed Lulu, her little old eyes deep in her face and close together, like a china doll.

"You can't. THIS is the hottest game in town. N, 40. En, four oh. Come join us. Just be on your best behavior. Do you have any of that?"

"Not much," giggled Lulu.

"Let me put chips on your card for the numbers we've already called. I, 19. I, one nine. Whew: who'd like to be nineteen again?"

Most shook their heads.

"Not me."

"Not me, neither."

"We get polished by life's sorrows, don't we?" I preached. "I, 29. I, two nine. We get better on the inside, the older these bodies get. Our hearts become more compassionate. Like living at this nursing home, here. How much PATIENCE have you each learned since you've been here? Now tell me, are you a better person now, or like you were twenty years ago?"

"Now," they mostly nodded.

"O, 68. Oh, six eight. Esther, you've got it: O, 68. Put a chip here. Shall I do it? Mabel, YOU are learning patience, aren't you?"

Mabel, of gracious manners and elegant warm hands, rolled her black eyes in wordless agreement. Just that morning, I knew, Mabel sat in her own excrement for an hour, because the nurses did not answer her bell. Then, as she was cleaned, she was scolded, and couldn't talk back. Mabel knew plenty about patience and humility. I moved around the table and gave her a kiss for bravery.

I regarded this nursing home stay as a tumbler for these people—to quickly rub off rough spots before they moved on— as a great opportunity for spiritual advancement. As their Jesus exhorted, here was the chance to turn the other cheek; to be the blessed meek who would inherit the kingdom of heaven. It was their time for their last spiritual sweetening, and I considered it my privilege to cheer them on in their work.

"I got married at 19," offered Sadie Lee.

"Did you wear white?"

"Nope. My Sunday go-to-meetin' suit, navy blue with tiny buttons all down the front of the jacket. Muh daddy made me drive the mules and plow since Ah was little. Ah wanted no more of that, so Ah run away and got married. My husband was half Cherokee," she boasted.

"THEN what did you do?"

"Drove HIS team of mules," Sadie chuckled.

"B, 12. Bee, twelve. Vitamin B12. Maybe I need some of that vitamin. Bee, One two. My hands are still cold. Ethel, may I just keep holding on? I never felt anything so satiny as Ethel's hands!" Ethel grunted and glowered, but kept her hand in mine.

"N, 36. En, three six. You've got it, Harry. Show him, Hazel. N, 36.

"Yep, it's colder up in the Upper Valley than it is down

here, Harry. And so much closer to those bluffs of the Topas.

"Once, my pal Wendy and I slept on top of those bluffs, on a rock twice the size of this table. We hardly slept all night, it was so beautiful. We could peer down over the edge from our sleeping bags and watch the birds circling beneath us and settling down into crevasses of the bluffs just below us. It was a full moon, and clean wind. Clouds strutted across the sky all night, and the moon reflected in the sea beyond Ventura, and the sunrise was in Technicolor, a whole flaming sky. I looked down across the valley to my house, and the little hilltop where I pray every morning. That's my church; and here I was sleeping on top of the steeple!

"O, 75. Oh, seven five. Mary, do you have a bingo? No?

"You remember what it feels like to be out there under the sky, don't you, Harry?"

"Fishin' up at the lakes," he managed in a hoarse whisper, although his mouth hung awry.

I grinned and loved him, knowing that I had enabled Harry to be vigorous up there in the Sierras for another moment, even while his body was stiffly here in the wheelchair.

"Bingo!" shouted Mary finally. But the prize from the bingo-box she offered to Sadie Lee. Without thanks, Sadie whipped the new beads over her head and wheeled out of the room, with a sly look of acquisition, as if she had just outfoxed someone. Mary just shook her head.

Chips clattered into their box, as I cleared the tables. I adjusted the seating for lunch, wheeled some of the people to other tables, as aides ushered Sadie Lee back in, and two other patients with hair wet from showering.

"The girls will be bringing you dinner in just a minute. Mmmm, smells like meatloaf. Thanks for the game."

As I left with my supplies under my arm, I paused at the door and grinned back at the perky faces all watching me, every one smiling.

Except Harry, whose mouth could not manage a smile—in fact was drooling, but his good hand lifted in salute, and his eyes were still dancing in mine.

And except for Mrs. Townsend, who had been moved from the mirror, but still looked astounded.

And except for Daisy Porter, who was asleep with her head on her hand, the skin of her bone face draping over the arm of the wheelchair.

Chapter 3

HEALTHY AGING
"Gettin' Good 'n' Old"

Before Mildred made it to 103, even in her late nineties, she was lamenting losing her eyesight. She could keep house, but she could no longer read sheet music. She had worked decades in a piano store, gifted with quick sight-reading, playing any piece of sheet music the first time she saw it. She had memorized nothing. Now at 98, all she could remember to play on her organ was "Happy Birthday."

I showed no sympathy. After all, she got to play music well into her 80's, but as a professional dancer, I got to dance for only 13 years and she didn't hear ME whining about it. Then I'd needle her with, "Look. At 98, your back is straight and tall, your posture is beautiful. You have no bone pain, and your mind is good. How could you live a century and not expect something to wear out?"

OLD ME

I, myself, have been shrinking since age 50. My bones are melting away within me. As another bent old neighbor said, I am turning into a jellyfish. They didn't warn us about bone pain. That I've discovered, is why we have 'cranky ole' ladies.' It's not envy. They don't want their youth back; they just want to stop hurting. Youth's emotional pain when driven by hormones was just as distracting as the ancients' bone pain. We leave one flavor of suffering and develop another. Perhaps old age, because of the aching hips, is the season for sitting comfortably and contemplating. We can be warm laps and good listeners while we contemplate.

I've lost my smeller too. A small loss, granted. Not the loss that eyesight is. Still, it's humiliating, because I never know when I or my home is offensive. I have no idea why people leave quickly when they drop by after my nice broccoli stir-fry lunch. Nor why my friends who know I have no "nose" secretly resent me when I drink their expensive wine.

But, we need to get a grip here. Vanity is the luxury of the young, and pure folly for the old. Aging bodies lose certain aptitudes. Everyone over 70 notices diminishing short-term memory, or word finding, or agility, or balance, or eyesight, or hearing, or smell and taste, or steady hands, or actual height, or the libido. Not to mention the treasured pucker factor that goes—causing us to drip into secret "pads" on the dance floor or in the grocery store. I do not get to pick which knack will abandon me. Let's make the best of it, finding faith, forbearance, and gratitude for what we retain.

See? I can still walk three miles a day, AND find my own way home. I can use the toilet AT WILL; and sleep when my head hits the pillow. My swallow still works and I read all I want and surf the web at 70, and I have patience for kids or puppies. Even though I cannot taste my dinner much, I can cook a healthy one. I fall on my face and skin my palms on the asphalt when I run. So I only walk, and gratefully.

The jackpot: aging has endowed me with a brand new gift, the I-don't-care syndrome, aka 'lazy-fair.' Catch me with my housedress inside out? Good, next time I put it on, it'll be right side out. Forget my favorite trolley driver's name? Doesn't matter, I remember and love his face. Make a fuss in the grocery line because I don't have my wallet, then find money in my other pocket? One time, a lady waited patiently behind me.

"That's OK, just a 'senior moment," she sympathized.

"Honey," I guffawed, "I don't have those anymore—now I only get 'junior moments.'" This new art of shamelessness, my favorite, goes with silly hats, ugly shoes, eating garlic, and naked armpits because their hair has migrated up to my chin. I'm retired, I rock a lot, and my little mistakes no longer matter!

"After all," it's fun to shrug with wide-eyed innocence, "I'm an old woman; I'm 70."

"I am 82 and I am not old yet!" protested the other carefully made-up woman on the trolley (whose lipstick was running into the age cracks around her mouth).

"Your choice," I retorted smugly through clean lips. "I get to be old at 70. I've earned it, I'm proud of it, I'm taking it easy. And I rock shamelessly."

I'm also adopting a second-hand dog, writing a book, and laughing a lot.

AGING IS A SPIRITUAL DISCIPLINE.

"Discipline?!!?"

Wait. Don't turn the page. Anything we do regularly to maintain life is a discipline. Eating is a discipline. Choosing the food for physical health is a discipline. Playing cards is a discipline to maintain mental and social health. Sleeping, practicing music, daily exercise, tithing, brushing teeth—our day is filled with disciplines. Including being kind to someone we do not like, cooking food for the family or the family shelter or Meals-On-Wheels, watering the yard, and caring for the animals. Even finding things funny is a discipline, for we know that life without laughter is not healthy life.

When we retire, driving and camping are disciplines, painting landscapes, volunteering, country dancing, water aerobics, gardening, too.

"Spiritual??"

We are all spiritual beings. There are three intertwined generic paths towards spiritual fulfillment: devotion, service, wisdom. The path of devotion means surrender to the Master; to love the Lord with all your heart and all your soul (Lord Jesus, Krishna, Buddha, the Guru) is a discipline. The path of service is the 'calling:' the surrender to the kinship of all, such as raising human children with health and integrity; the calling to the priesthood or nunnery; teaching or healing or feeding human beings; protecting the planet and its creatures; or managing wealth altruistically, etc. is a discipline. The path of wisdom, surrender to the Truth or the Way eternal with contemplation, prayer or meditation, is a discipline. We begin on one path, no matter what our religion or tradition may be, and if we advance, we can eventually, naturally, embrace all three paths—braided together.

Any attainment requires self-discipline. The violinist and the carpenter and the ice-skater begin practice in childhood. The practice of spiritual skills generally seems to take over in later life.

Spiritual discipline could be anything we do that reduces selfishness. Austerity of dress and food and dwelling, silence, non-wasting of water, non-polluting of air, sharing of riches, prayer, contemplation, meditation, accepting psychotherapy, reading, listening, chastity, simplicity, humility, detachment, generosity, tolerance. Might not old age be the perfect opportunity to practice these disciplines? Is that not what retirement is about? To settle into the quiet life, or the life of serving the community, or the life of contemplating creation through art or travel or study? To pass on family treasures and history to the youth? To clean out one's life, make amends, express gratitude?

And if we skip the disciplines of old age, perhaps the austerity of a nursing home is the fast-track for catching up, for letting go. And the pain in these old bones, the humiliations, the confinement, might serve to goad us on. Healthy old age is our last and best opportunity for improving as human beings.

Ponder the concept of HEALTHY AGING. An oxymoron, you say? Have a look at the losses and gains of aging in a century of life:

PHYSICALLY, it is true, we lose. We peak out in the first bloom of adulthood, say in our second or third decade. But as we approach ten decades, one hundred years, that is 36,500 days of working, digesting, excreting, pumping blood, with 6,307,200 inhalations and 42,048,000 heartbeats. The system is bound to wear out.

Why, tell me WHY, does this surprise us? We begin our century, owning only a nipple; we accrue grand possessions and territories, then finish up the century once again without control over anyone or anything, even our own bowels. Yes, age means physical loss. But what about the mind and heart and soul part of this fabulous human being?

INTELLECTUALLY, we can peak out mid-century, and then keep our knowledge, ability to learn and solve, our reason and logic. After many decades of life's experiences, we are 'the wiser for wear'—which, boiled down, means we've finally learned to be quiet and listen and observe and be in awe. Hence, in most cultures, the age-old reverence for counselors, for our wise elders.

PSYCHO-SOCIALLY, we peak out in old age. We begin as infants by loving only the bearer of the nipple, then reaching to the other parent, siblings, schoolmates, nation, finally we mature into embracing the planet and all its beings. That caring comes with healthy aging, and it need not diminish.

SPIRITUALLY, folks, it just gets better and better. If we die well, we are at our very best when we take our last breath. Life is a series of changes, losses—we plummet, and pick ourselves up, grieve and heal, over and over again, each time building new spiritual muscles. A roller coaster whose dips and climbs keep getting higher and higher. We become contemplatives at retirement, thoughtfully counting out the sandwiches for meals-on-wheels, quiet on the golf course, rocking a child, fishing at the lake, solitary in our painting or woodwork out in the garage, reading scriptures all week long, or praying at odd moments even when we are not desperate. All of that is meditation; we can ignore our aching bones, while our spirit expands and soars.

So as you age, get a grip. Shrug at the sagging flesh, and thrill at your wise, kind, peaceful self, your real self.

Nobody wants to talk about aging. They actually think 'aging' is a negative word, and chide me for being a spoilsport. Instead of avoiding it, how about admitting to the sequences of bloating and shriveling of an aging body, while simultaneously appreciating that the wisdom, compassion, spirit—the heart of us—grows better and better with age. I think of aging as maturing, like fine wine or a windswept mountain. Of course, wine might become vinegary, but that is an accident, and not fine aged wine. A human can have accidents, such as a cerebral-vascular accident (stroke) or other damage that causes dementia. Please remember that stroke and dementia do not mean old, they mean damaged 'n' old. Old by itself means good 'n' old. So let us notice that while the body gets older, the soul gets bolder. Let us notice that our life span is a full century now, acknowledge that we are growing very old, and take stock.

Instead of wasting our energy on outraged indignation when our eyesight fades, our memory falters, and the hips ache—we can take that walker in our stride and smile. We can let that 'dirty old man' and that 'nagging old shrew' fade away, and we can shine with the capacity to be...HONEST, RESPONSIBLE, TRUSTING, GENEROUS, DECENT elders.

Sounds like a Boy Scout's oath? Actually, these virtues take on a different twist when we use them regarding aging well, regarding being less of a burden to our kinfolk, regarding the dignity, importance, and the fun of being the tribal ancients:

HONEST

In an old person, HONESTY means no more baking the turkey or driving to Minnesota, no more facelifts or Viagra. It means dropping euphemisms like 'senior citizen' and luxuriating in the power and authority of the words 'old man' and 'old woman.' It means having the courageous honesty to face facts: "In the last decade of my long life I cannot physically do it all myself, any more than I could in the first decade." To say to people, "OK, it's your turn. You can do it for me, and you deserve to be compensated." The family ancient has earned the right to be served by others, in whatever small ways might be necessary, and to be honest enough to allow it. To be honest enough to notice when he has outlived his ability to take total care of himself! The honesty to acknowledge and accept the need for assistance as a part of the natural life span! And rather than lament it, to embrace it, and enjoy it. The honesty to rest on your laurels, knowing that you deserve that rest, that it's your turn to be the recipient of the kindness of others. After a lifetime of doing kindness, it is only just. Picture that old man, strolling through the forest, steadying himself with his hand on the shoulder of his grandson who is describing to him his recent experiences in boot camp. Or the old woman seated, proudly witnessing her great-granddaughter's prom-dress fitting. So relent, be proudly HONEST about your age, and take it easy.

RESPONSIBLE

As the healthy family elder, you can be fully RESPONSIBLE for yourself, for your social, spiritual, financial well-being, as well as fully RESPONSIBLE for the care of your body—bathing, trimming, exercising, feeding, and bedding it down. But who will continue when you cannot? It is your responsibility to assign others to take care of things for you when you are unable. Your responsibility is to enable others to manage your affairs! "My funeral choices are duly recorded," you might protest.

Good! In fact many of us have made friends with that 'd' word (DEATH). It has become the fashion among enlightened seniors to prepare their wills or trusts, funeral arrangements, even their Advance Directives. Elizabeth Kübler-Ross started that when she invented death and dying! But even she wasn't prepared for that last decade of her life. She had overlooked that other 'd' word (DEPENDENCY). After her stroke, she became a bitter and disillusioned woman until she finally recognized that unconditional love applied to loving herself, no matter what, as well.

Have you made arrangements for that dependence which comes before your last breath?? Where is the money to pay for your care? Is the house to be mortgaged? Or sold? Or the Hummel figurines and family silver? Or will you expect kinfolk to move in and nurse you? How eligible are you for governmental assistance? What does your insurance cover?

What if you were called far away temporarily, tomorrow, perhaps to tend to a dying uncle who would take months to die? Can everything be managed while you are out of town, or out of commission? What if you were suddenly hospitalized for many weeks? Or traumatized by an auto accident? Have you made arrangements for a trusted person to run your household? If some vascular problem caused you to become very forgetful—you might indignantly slap any hand offered to you. Under any of those circumstances, someone might have to come in and manage your affairs for a while. But they cannot, without previously granted permission.

Have you empowered anyone of a younger generation to pay your bills, water the dog and the lawn, make and keep your appointments for you, pour the white stuff into your septic tank? Have you cleared away your obsolete junk and useless papers, making accessible the necessary information, so that they CAN help you?

You need to assign who is to care for you when you cannot— temporarily OR permanently—and empower them legally and financially and morally, so that they can. Get that second signature on your checking account, or Power of Attorney, as well as Durable Power of Attorney for Health Care, or Advance Directive, so they can manage your affairs according to your explicit wishes and under your auspices. Then look them in the eye and talk to them about all this!!

TRUSTING

So, when you sit down eye-to-eye and speak with your 'youngers' about your own future, what do you say?

"I TRUST you."

If you outlive your abilities, most likely you will not be aware of it. But your family or doctor or neighbor will see the dirty shirt, the rotten food in the fridge, the weight you are losing, or the dehydration that renders you weak and frequently on the floor. Someone else will have to take the reins, to see that you are properly cared for. You can find the strength to say it now:

"I TRUST you to take over and make the right decisions when I have lost my own good judgment and can no longer live alone."

While of sound mind, now, my fellow aging person, you must bestow TRUST on someone—TRUST of your younger helper to seek the best for you 'when the time comes.' Whether your caregivers-to-be are family or hired people; whether they come to your house, or you move into their house; whether you can afford your own personal caregivers, or you must share the cost of help with others in a group home; whether it be in a family home or in an assisted living facility—however it will be best arranged then, you cannot possibly predict now. So you must TRUST that when the time comes, whether you are cooperating or resisting them, that your youngers will make the best decisions possible.

For example, now you would never intrude on your daughter's household, but then maybe she will be single and needing the extra income your care-giving pays. Or she might have moved into a house with an adjoining granny flat, or just down the street from a charming retirement home, where your private room with your beautiful things in it and round-the-clock helpers awaits you. Or maybe the kid married wealth and needs no inheritance, so she can mortgage your home and pay for all the personal attention you will be craving. TRUST her now, look her in the eye and grant that forgiveness for carrying through on the most difficult chore of her life—bucking you, taking over, being the grown-up, making tough choices. And thank her profusely, now.

There are many times in life when we are forced to close our eyes, grit our teeth, and jump off that high diving board. Jumping into a marriage, quitting a job, buying a house, sending the child to camp, accepting psychotherapy from a stranger, adopting a rescue dog, and allowing others to care for us, are all risky. Not the least of these is trusting a 15-year-old to grow up and do right by you. But often that is your best option. And trust you must. Prepare to surrender yourself to the decisions of the youths you have chosen to empower.   Instead of becoming a cranky, unwittingly smelly burden and being placed by the courts in a facility of their choice; instead of breaking a hip and winding up in the three-bed ward of a noisy nursing home—allow yourself the option of spending a few cozy years under minimal supervision, with the comfort of your own belongings around you and the sweet bits of freedom you can still enjoy. (Yes, you can be cagey and divide up the control—one grandkid has Power of Attorney, another is named on Advanced Directives, another is the Trustee of your estate, another's name is on the house, etc.) Have faith in the universe, in God, in karma, in the family values you have taught … whatever, have faith. Bite that bullet again and mean it when you say,

"I TRUST you."

Then TRUST. And lighten up and take it easy.

GENEROUS

The healthiest aging person is the most GENEROUS one. Generous? Lavishing store-bought stuff and bank accounts on others? No, think more of a gracious kind person, of a GENEROSITY OF SPIRIT. A generosity that graciously receives, a generosity that gives trust, responsibility, confidence and power to another person.

"I don't want to be a burden" can be a stingy statement. It sounds thoughtful but it often means "I want to be in control, I will accept nothing from anybody, I will not give you my respect, nor empower you."

An extremely GENEROUS elder I know, my mother Janet, would accept everything with delight and gratitude: a brand-new day from beyond the foot of her bed, a cut rose from the desk clerk, a game of rummy from the grandson, a ride to the store from a neighbor.

After seventy years of driving, it takes an act of GENEROSITY to relinquish the car, to leave the lanes for those who know which one they want—to allow the restrictions and the dependency upon others by graciously accepting rides.

It is actually 'more blessed' to receive than to give, because you are generously allowing others the opportunity to give. Do you remember receiving that ugly clay hand-print ashtray from your proud kindergartner, as if it were a diamond? The best relationships work when folks are receiving as well as giving. Think about good sex, the successful marriage, raising confident children—the best moments happened when you empowered another by receiving from him/her.

That same GENEROUS receptivity is essential for the dependent family elder. So in our fifties, we need to start the conscious practice of occasionally letting others do for us, to practice the knack of receiving. Occasionally? I mean weekly, folks, not annually. Are you balking? The depth of your resistance now is equal to the rigidity of your recalcitrance when you are very old.

It takes humility to receive. Listening is a most generous act, to openly receive the meaning of the speaker. To hear out the joke and give genuine laughter. To listen to the problems and hear the unspoken fears and doubts behind the words. The family elder is the family receiver, the sponge soaking up the ills, the lap for the child, the observant person, available to hear the troubles and triumphs of others, the wise counselor of the family. Professional counselors, in this culture of dis-membered families, are the temporary substitutes for our family elders, the listening, wise, family elders, the no-longer-self-involved, the seen-it-all-been-there-done-that, compassionate, GENEROUS, family elders. Let the youngers 'produce.' Let the youngers take the credit. Let the youngers be active and too busy to stop and listen. They should be able to turn to their 'non-productive' elders for solace and encouragement, for someone they can talk to and laugh with, for 'someone who understands.'

And these are the healthy-minded elders who will let the kids do things for them. And when they allow others to do for them without resistance, they are NOT a burden, and it becomes a pleasure and a privilege to serve them. And THAT IS MOST GENEROUS.

DECENT

What is a DECENT old man? A DECENT old woman? No spitting, defecating, nor disrobing in public? Granted. Plus, DECENCY to die in timely manner.

WHAT??!

Now, hold on: suicide and euthanasia are totally out of the question. Why? They are not necessary. We don't need them. We know how to die. In fact we die the moment we are ready.

But some people protest that they are ready to die and not dead yet, so they think they must cause trauma to the body to get out of it. That is a lie. The mouth might say, "I'm ready to die," but the will to live is still keeping body and soul intact. And how do I know that, in spite of your protests, you are not ready to die? Because you are still breathing, still eating, still complaining. Richard Bach said, in *Illusions*, "Here's a test to find whether your mission on earth is finished. If you are alive, it isn't." The moment people are ready to go, all on their own, they stop breathing. That is how we know they were ready.

But you insist on euthanasia because you don't want pain? Get hospice! They will keep you out of pain until you die, exactly as you request, even if it takes putting you into deep sleep. You will only last a few days that way, dying naturally from lack of food and fluids. (Hospice knows that the body naturally declines food and drink during the dying process, and has found that while dying, natural starvation is cleansing and euphoric; that while dying, natural dehydration—although it causes dry-mouth for which they suggest sucking on ice chips—is a natural analgesic which reduces pain.) With hospice you give yourself time to ease out. Which gives your people time to let go of you. The apple falls from the tree when it is ready, and when the tree is in season.

So, how to die? Keep ready. Clean closets. Pitch junk. Clear the heart of resentments and clear the mind of itches—such as, just one more back rub, just one more command to my servile spouse, just wait until my estranged brother comes, just one more Guinness, or one more Thanksgiving ... The body has its own wisdom, knows how to shut down, knows when the fruit is fully ripe, whether age 9 or 90. All we need to do is respect that and let it do its thing.

I find it so very simple: never cause my dying, plus, never prolong my dying. Dying is NOT failure, nor crime. Dying is just the next step. Dying is a natural, major project, and must be allowed its time. So I have already started preparing to refuse food and medical treatment when they become counter-productive to my own dying process.

Make it clear in your end-of-life document just what you want for yourself when a terminal illness or injury takes over. Remember that every little thing the medical profession does to you, they cannot do without signed permission. It seems silly to go for open-heart surgery when your body is already giving out with MS, or to radically attempt cancer cure when you have used up the time your body can tolerate kidney dialysis. Why prolong life of part of the body (which medicine promises to manage) while another part is irreversibly wearing out (beyond medical capabilities)? Why cure pneumonia when the brain isn't working right? Why do open heart surgery on a woman's body that is otherwise dying of multiple sclerosis, or Lou Gehrig's disease?

For decent old age, stay current with yourself, keep peace daily with your world, with those around you. Live humbly and simply as your age and infirmities dictate, delve into your spiritual recesses, savor your own personal lifetime history, find forgiveness—for others and for yourself, and say goodbye to it all with each evening prayer. Hopefully, when the time comes to die you will not dig in your heels, and you can slip away, as one scripture says, 'like stealing perfume from the flowers.' We can die easily, peacefully, without a big scuffle, without much ado.

A master 'die-er' was Gramp, in a beautiful photo essay by his grandsons.* Living in his family's rural home, his life riddled with Alzheimer's, one day at the dinner table, half naked because he couldn't remember how his pants worked, Gramps handed his false teeth to his grandson.

"Here, you can have these; I won't be needing them anymore," he declared. Gramps never ate again and quietly died a few weeks later.

So the DECENT elder is one who is ready to heed the words of Marcus Aurelius in Meditations (AD 160):

> **Thou hast embarked.**
> **Thou hast made the voyage.**
> **Thou art come to shore.**
> **Get out.**

Once we are ready, death is a quiet event, a simple moment. Many an old person have I seen generously grace their family with a quick and easy death, a tidy death, as simple as blowing out a candle, leaving their loved ones strangely exhilarated.

It is in our capacity to do so.

Gramp, by Mark Jury and Dan Jury, 1978, Grossman Publishers

HOMEWORK-7: Collect facts needed for your obituary - the simple factual one required by funeral directors; add to your Vital Info files (see Appendix 6 for further guidelines).

ITEMS FOR OBITUARY

- *Full name, maiden name, of deceased, place and date of birth, place and date and time of death, cause of death*
- *Parents' full names, names at birth if different, state of birth*
- *Siblings, full names, location*
- *Offspring, full names, location*
- *Marriages, if divorced or widowed*
- *Last year of school, place/certificate*
- *Primary occupations*
- *Club memberships*
- *Honors/awards/recognitions*
- *Military service/branch/dates*

FUN TO BE FAT

I first noticed it was fun to be fat when I handed my deposit to the bank teller. When I leaned against the counter I bounced back as if it were rubber. It felt as if someone from behind me had slipped a cushion between me and the counter. I looked around and no one was there. I looked down to see the cushion, and it was just ME there. Quite there. I giggled. I glanced around the room to see if anyone else had noticed. Of course, they weren't paying me any attention. Then I began to realize that I was a walking collection of cushions—as if I went to sleep at age 61 and woke up at 62 with someone else's body on me. I had no idea they could do full body transplants nowadays.

I like my new body. It is rounded all over. Not a bone in sight. You have no idea how embarrassed I was years ago when I would try to cuddle my newborn infant and his head would clunk against my clavicle. I was all clavicles. And the armpits! I always wore long sleeves as a professional dancer—when you raise your arms to dance, the pits are not supposed to be hollow as teacups. When your arms rest on your pillow around your head, like fallen silk, after making love, they should be sensuous, not emaciated.

In Spain, my husband and his family pitied me for my ugliness, not so much because of the freckles, but because of the skinniness. It looked like poverty to them. He relished women who were sumptuously endowed, with healthy meat on them. No, we're not talking morbid obesity here, but rather a concept of beauty a hundred years behind ours—the standards of Renoir and Degas and the classicists. And suddenly now, I have attained that wanted loveliness. Bowed thighs of anorexic women, with light coming through them as they walk towards you, are as pitiful as the thighs of premature infants. I am pleased with my middle-aged abundance.

In our youth, slender is more natural. In full womanhood—childbearing age, breasts full of milk, handy hips for carrying children—maturing of flesh is appropriate. Then at grandmother-age, our job is to be a lap, a little guy's sofa, with cushions all over us, and a rocking chair to set them in while we sing lullabies. You do not have any children to cuddle? Yes, you do, just look around. The neighbor's latchkey kids, the babies in the hospital ward, all our children nowadays with two working parents and not enough attention. (Do you remember saying, "Mommy, lookee, lookee!" And she did?) Find anybody's child and offer the advantage of your comfy lap to nurture them.

I do not worry a bit about having gained a third of my weight in my 60's. It is temporary. Soon enough, in my late 70's or 80's, I will raisin up. Most elders shrivel down to wrinkled skin hanging on bones. (Never mind, raisins are even sweeter than grapes.) Much easier to navigate those old bones for the time being, and then less to bury when the time comes. The body has its own wisdom—skinny at both birth and death simply means less for other folks to carry.

For now, it is fun to be fat, to glimpse a Renoir painting in the mirror. If you do not believe me, rent the movie "Baghdad Café," and watch a nakedly beautiful, well-cushioned, healthy specimen of middle-aged sensuality. It is delightful.

In short, let us be just the age we are, and be glad.

ODE TO A WHEELED CHAIR

"I'll never get in one of those things!"

Can you believe it? There are people so superstitious, so fearful, so prejudiced about WHEELCHAIRS they refuse to sit in one, if only to see how beautifully it works!

Back when I worked at the nursing home, I held wheelchair races. We cleared the halls. Staff, aides, patients, and family members raced each other. It was fun! Lulu, age 79, beat us all. She proudly displayed her blue ribbon above her bed, bragging about it for the rest of her life. And that is how we all learned what clever vehicles they were, and that if you use a wheelchair, you are merely a regular person sitting in a chair on wheels, propelling it yourself—where and when you want to. A wheelchair means freedom. Never blame IT for your future confinement, your injury, your frail old age. It is a good companion, a friend, and a RELEASE from confinement.

In India, I have seen many a person scooting along on a makeshift board with skate-wheels, or using elbows as crutches, loping along the ground like a crab. In Spain, years ago, the only wheelchair I saw was a wicker chair lashed to tiny wheels—a VERY ROUGH ride along unpaved village roads.

Why this superstition, as if once in it we will stick to it? Folks, it is only a seat—a wheelchair is not an appendage. It is an elegant vehicle, common only in an affluent society. And it is simply a place to sit while you are on the go. Like a car. A car is not a wart on your behind, either. Yes, the doctor warns that if you get lazy with a wheelchair and don't get all the exercise you can, you will be stuck in it. The same can be said of the couch that 'potato' is sunk in, yet we do not fear the couch!

We do not have any fear of a bicycle—another vehicle to get somewhere, also with big wheels to make the ride smoother and easier to propel. And a bicycle has its shortcomings—you cannot ride it indoors, cannot turn it around on a dime, cannot back it up to the toilet. Not to SPEAK of the torture of that little tiny saddle in your crotch. Yet no one fears a bicycle!

Your COMFORTABLE wheeled chair has its own two steering wheels – one for each of its smooth ball bearing wheels, so you can steer it and propel it with a light touch. (And both can be mounted on one side, if you can use only one hand.) The steering wheel is slightly smaller than the rubber tire, so that it locomotes VERY easily, yet does not touch the ground—staying clean for your hands. The wheelchair has back-handles so someone can push it for you. That back-seat driver can easily press on the back foot bar to raise your small front wheels up over a curb—also with little effort.

And have you seen those wheeled basketball teams on TV? They don't have back-seat driver equipment on their small, very light, Maserati-like set of wheels. Those guys 'pop wheelies' (rearing up on their big back wheels) to turn on a dime; using their great balance and powerful arms, they fly around to win many a game. Their chairs are their freedom, and I bet they keep them as tuned as a race car.

A wheelchair means you can do more, join in more, get out of the house more, shop longer without getting tired, enjoy museums for hours, keep up with your legged companions, and race down airport runways to catch that flight.

When we took our elders to the Getty Museum, my 88-year-old mother gamely sat in a nice wheelchair. (They had rows and rows of them for us to sign out like library books). At times she pushed her empty chair, using it like her walker. And sometimes she was pushing me in it. (That is how EASY they are to push!) She kept up with us and never got tired. Her boyfriend refused to use one. He was a drag, slowed us down, made us choose shorter routes and clip our tour short.

Next time, of course, we left the boyfriend home, confined to his pride and prejudice. And we requested two wheelchairs—one for mom and one for me. It was fun. Except that my son and I kept bickering over mine. I didn't WANT to take turns.

HOMEWORK-8: Wheelchair day with friend to a museum or shopping, strolling around a park. Take turns in the chair with your friend, at least a half hour each. Notice how the one in the chair gets no eye contact from passersby. Then vow to give eye contact and friendliness to everyone you pass in a wheelchair, giving the same respect you give to those standing, and notice if it changes your attitude about this wonderful vehicle.

JANET

At 88, Janet was happy. She had progressed from big home to smaller homes—cleaning out garages and closets as the stuff became obsolete. She had left her last home voluntarily, to be nearer her family. She had sold her car and used the money to pay for good help. Once again, her home was just the size she could manage—now a studio apartment, furnished with her family treasures—the Victorian love-seat, the grandfather clock, Hummel figures, and an antique pitcher full of cut roses people loved to bring her. The crystal went to her niece, china to her sister; she gave her stainless steel to her daughter and kept her wedding sterling for everyday use.

She slipped little gifts—still paring down her belongings—to the girls who cleaned her place. She enjoyed her supper company in the gracious dining room of the retirement home where everyone seemed to know her, and she made bets over which waitress was pregnant. Janet had no more time for sewing because she was 'too busy'—snoozing in her recliner, or watching the birds catching the drafts of the storm clouds over the water beyond, or bickering over seed on her balcony garden.

Oh, but you should have tasted her delicious corn pancakes. And you should have heard her swear, or chuckle at dirty old lady jokes! She sparkled. She wore clothes that once belonged to her deceased baby sister, beautiful colors, with a smile that lit up the room. She liked the young man who helped her set up her funeral plans, just as she doted on her grandson when he picked up milk or bananas for her. You should have seen her in her backwards baseball cap, driving a 'Lil' Indy' bumper car behind his!

She often obeyed the doctors who oversaw her various body parts. She lived around her bowel issues and her back pain. She gamely sat in that wheelchair to tour the Getty Museum, in order to keep pace with her family. Bragging over the popcorn and cocoa she proudly served out of her kitchenette, Janet cheated and gloated at backgammon. She aged with laughter: slowing down nicely, becoming more frail, unsteady, and surprisingly mellow.

Janet had been so much fun dancing the Charleston and the Balboa, back when, that her friends called her 'Jazzbo.' Her daughter had fun with her again, still called her 'Jazzbo' and bragged about her at the senior center, because Janet was not only a delight but a model of healthy aging. She accepted appropriate help with admirably good humor. Although her sphere of activity was drastically reduced, she enjoyed what she did, she enjoyed where she lived, and she enjoyed who she was. Her griefs were grieved; her affairs were in order. And she had evenings to reminisce over her life with her boyfriend, who was 94 and thrilled to know her.

MY STYLE

I have no intention of growing old in Janet's style. I laud her skills, but I do not have them. Nor do I have her assets. Neither will I have kinfolk to run interference, 'look after me' when I am her age. In fact, I don't intend to reach her age. I expect to wear out sooner.

Janet sports quite an impressive medical history. I get no particular pleasure out of visiting a bevy of medical practitioners and technicians, so I am not a steady customer, and I intend to ignore most of their offers in the future. As I age, I will forego life-extending procedures at an accelerating rate. So, as I approach the depletion of my brain and bone, and the end of my NATURAL born days, I hope to be really ready to go. In my 60's, I hoped to retire, explore some new pursuits (music, writing, volunteering), enjoy my friends, and play. In my 70's, I am writing energetically. In my 80's I hope to become more retiring, pull in my flaps (get rid of belongings and projects other than the spiritual One), to walk and rock and watch my green trees, and pray, and open my heart towards the Light of my life.

Then I will let the chips fall where they may. For whatever illness comes along, I can allow comfort measures only and refuse curative treatment (such as antibiotics, surgery, dialysis, chemotherapy). Then, if appetite or ability to eat wanes, it will be my opportunity to quit eating in the natural course of things. And then, with grace, luck, good legal documents, good preparations, and the best of intentions, not to speak of kind people, I hope to die in timely manner, at peace.

*HOMEWORK-9: Examine your own life's goals
from where you stand now:
1) How would you want to live each of three future
decades? OR 2) If you had six months left to live,
how would you spend them?*

Chapter 4

DEMENTIA

"Do You Remember You Forgot?"

MEMORY LOSS

Memory loss is the part of aging that will not happen to me! I've never had much memory to lose. Forgetting is a talent I was born with, and I have become quite an expert as I have matured. You could say, at 60 I am precocious. I expect to die a master.

My saving grace is, I still remember that I forget. It has not quite entered the realm of dementia – at which time I will deny ever having forgotten a thing. That could come, I suppose. For now, suffice it that I still have good judgment. That is, I can be trusted to not trust myself. Usually.

A while back, I attended a National Hospice Teleconference in a nearby city. I heard an interesting Buddhist chaplain speak. Next day as I left my house for my morning walk, that same chaplain passed me in his car and said, "Hi, Susie!" He knew my name! I actually hadn't told him my name at the conference. And what brought him so far over here?

"Oh! Hello, uh...," I smiled, trying to remember his name from the program. "Do you live around here?"

"Yes," he replied helpfully, "I'm your next door neighbor."

Oops.

But introductions had been only once and soooo unremarkable. . .

And last month, I ran over my lunch. I was astonished, of course. When I felt the wheels bump over something, I wondered what it

57

could be and I stopped my car in the middle of the street to look back. Fascinating. I watched my olives roll down the driveway. I had no idea who left my lunch there (I live alone). Later, people in the kitchen of the senior center stood gaping at me like looky-loos at a crime scene while I washed off my lunch. I figured anyone who runs over her lunch deserves to eat it. However I did not drink the orange juice. When I packed it, it had been in the orange.

Of course, years ago, I wisely gave up locking my car. It was always so expensive to get my keys out of it. No, I am not afraid of car theft. I figure if they want it, they can have it. After losing your memory, a car is small potatoes. And, of course, it is stolen about once a week. I leave work at the end of a busy day to find my favorite parking spot EMPTY and my heart pounds. I swallow hard, pray it is not so, then search. I find that car parked in the darnedest places...

Trouble is, forgetting does not always help you forget the embarrassment of having forgotten. And people are so helpful to remind me. My extremely infrequent memory lapses provide for some people a hearty laugh, or the satisfaction of superiority, and for others the relief of kinship.

I felt pretty exposed, some years ago, after driving out from under a shoebox full of cassette tapes I had left on top of my car. I fled the seemingly irate driver who kept honking at me until he cornered me in the grocery parking lot, trying to inform me that my tapes had fallen off at the traffic light a few blocks back. I lurched back on two wheels to retrieve them. Too late! Their plastic cases were crunched like sparkling ice chips in the main street of town, at rush hour, the cassette tape spaghetti blowing around the highway with the gust of each passing car. I reeled it all in, miles of the stuff, while plucking shards of plastic and dodging cars. Of course everyone I knew drove by and waved and grinned. Friendly town.

So, next time you cannot find your glasses, which you have pushed up onto your head, just be grateful you have not sat on them, like some of us do.

FORGETFULNESS

When we are physically exhausted, the brain is one of the first organs to show that it is just plain pooped. Like, after a day of intense shopping, Mom would say, "I'm so tired I can't think straight. I can't even remember my own name."

Bereavement causes emotional, physical, mental depletion. A bereaved person is mentally fatigued, and typically quite forgetful. In fact, any crisis, any stress, causes forgetfulness.

Perhaps that forgetfulness is often just a protection, to keep us from trying to do what we are just too depleted to manage anyway.

In the aging process, there are all kinds of reasons for becoming forgetful. Basically, our physical system slowly wears out with age. And our brain is a tired physical organ. Fading eyesight in some physical bodies, hearing loss in others, or back-outta-whack, and most of all, mild forgetfulness, are very common as we age.

I like to think of my old brain as a computer hard drive with no more 'bytes' left on it. I can still remember the stuff that HAS been recorded, but not much more GETS recorded nowadays. And that is annoying. Embarrassing. But it is not alarming.

So when should we be alarmed about poor memory? When are our 'forgets' warning signs of a developing dementia? Like Alzheimer's? A progressive atrophying of the brain, and a terminal illness, Alzheimer's IS alarming.

We are probably OK until we have cognitive loss. That is, until we not only forget what, we also forget how. For example: It is OK if your husband forgets to pick up some butter on the way home, but he is in trouble if he can no longer find his way home. You forget your friend's name when introducing her, so what, but it is a problem if you no longer can make and keep a luncheon date. You can forget your baby grandchild was coming over, but once he is there, if you no longer can remember to keep him safe, you are both in trouble. You forget to turn off the iron, common occurrence, but the problem is when you store it in the freezer.

In a senior moment, you might forget to serve your rolls at your dinner party, but it is dementia if you can no longer organize the dinner. It is normal to have trouble finding a word, but it is Alzheimer's if you substitute inappropriate words, turning your sentence into gibberish. We all forget our doctor's appointments, but we still know how to find his office. You can forget which day of the week it is or where you are going for a moment, as long as you do not become lost on your own street, or on your way to your own bathroom. Any healthy senior can forget her keys, but it is dementia if she cannot unlock the door of the public restroom.

Someone said, "If you remember forgetting, that's OK. If you forget you forgot, that's not."

Personally, I have always been forgetful—perhaps as self-defense when things got overwhelming. And it waxes and wanes with stress. However, as long as I can apologize later, and I still balance my checkbook, change a light bulb, and get my blouse on right side out, I am good enough.

HOWEVER, I have also mapped out for myself what to do if Alzheimer's comes along. Preparation has reduced my dread. Want to do that for yourself? It took me many days of concentration to get hold of my fear and put these thoughts down on paper. Making a plan felt like prayer for me. And I have not given it another thought. Others claim that reading it has encouraged them, so I include it here. Do write your own; your solutions might not be the same as mine. Of course the object is not merely to seek solutions, but also the process of facing the worst and overcoming your fear (See Appendix 8).

> *HOMEWORK-10: Discuss with a loved one or pal how you each would want to be cared for in the event your body were well and able while your brain developed dementia. The more sincere you are, the harder it is. Be brave.*

Chapter 5

"ARE YOUR AFFAIRS IN ORDER?"
"Well, Are YOURS?"

NOT FOR THE ELDERLY

These admonishments on aging well are NOT directed towards the elderly. By then it's too late. You and I can get ready before we grow old.

Once your kids are grown, out of the house, making children of their own; or once you are enjoying your fifties and their liberation from all those lusts, drives, and fears of young adulthood (oh hallelujah!) or once you have reached the calm maturity of your middle years; then these tips on aging nicely are for YOU. It takes years of practice to become a great cellist, a great chess player, or a great FAMILY ELDER.

Start practicing NOW the skills you need for successful aging. Start preening your psyche now towards the goals, towards the wisdom of healthy old age. Clean out that garage. Label and sort the photos for the kids. Get your affairs in order—NOW. My goal was to have it all done by my 60th birthday. I did pretty well, but I didn't finish.

"But," you protest, "my old folks should be getting their affairs in order too!" Right you are. So how do you get them to do it? BY DOING YOUR OWN. Your Will, your Vital Index, your Durable Power of Attorney for Healthcare, your trusted youngers empowered in case you become impaired day after tomorrow itself—there are 21 items you need to attend to, listed below.

You do your job, to help your youngers; only then can you look your elders in the eye and request they do the same to help you. If you tell the old folks what they should do, you'll get nowhere. But if you come on as the ignorant, worried kid (which you are) who needs their guidance on what they want you to do, the kid who needs their instructions—you might just get some answers.

I visited a gentleman who described himself as terminally ill and "wouldn't last until Christmas."

"Are your affairs in order?" I helpfully asked.

He responded indignantly, "Well, are YOURS?"

Phew! Was he calling my hypocrisy! Did I think that my life was not a terminal dis-ease?!

Luckily I could respond:

"Well, I know I want to be cremated. How about you, Mary?" And his wife said that she wanted burial in the family plot back home.

Then, and only then, was he willing to review his own affairs and set them straight.

So, are YOUR affairs in order? No time like the present to start tidying up, organizing, reducing, simplifying, clarifying, your own personal matters and possessions. When you clean out that garage, you clean out your emotional baggage. Updating your financial and legal affairs helps you face your own mortality, which enables you to better stand by and comfort your fellow mortals.

Believe it or not, planning your funeral can make you a better friend. Yes. And a happier person.

MY AFFAIRS IN ORDER

Ever since my hospice patient asked me if my affairs were in order, I have been working on them. What are 'affairs'? Well, there are many: financial affairs, social affairs, household business, emotional resolutions, spiritual balance sheet. My goal was to have everything in order by age 60. I succeeded somewhat, but realized that it is actually a work in progress as long as I live. So every few years, I weed out, update, and refresh things. (For examples, my baby sister, who was to care for me in my senility, has died ahead of me; and my emptied storage closet has filled up again.) As I discuss this list of 'affairs' with other people, they add items, and it keeps growing. Here is my latest version:

LIST OF AFFAIRS TO PUT IN ORDER

- Second signature on checking account, or Power of Attorney.
- Index of Vital Info—on self, dependents, and pets. And copies to those who might need them. And update it annually.
- Disposition and funeral preferences expressed, registered, or paid.
- Durable Power of Attorney for Healthcare, aka Advance Directive.
- Will, and/or Living Trust, and/or TOD (Transfer on Death for investments).
- Assets listed, valued, clarified—taught to survivors.
- Verbal permission, apology, gratitude, and forgiveness, to chosen youngers, NOW while of sound mind, for when you can no longer live alone and they must take over your decision-making and see that you get the care you need.
- List possible care facilities (assisted living, nursing homes, etc.) for future use, with reasons for your preferences. Add to Index of Vital Info file.
- Learn now to receive, to relinquish control/power (practice letting others wait on you!)
- Cherished belongings listed or labeled.
- Procedures and prices for selling valuables (vehicles, jewelry, antiques).
- Dump obsolete possessions. Clean out garage, closet, address book, computer files.
- Confidential papers/diaries/photos—properly disposed of.
- Family photos sorted, labeled, and dispersed amongst youngers.

- Reduce dwelling to fit your needs and abilities.
- Keep home repaired—towards sale or widowhood.
- Teach spouse, or write instructions for, your household jobs: finances, laundry, cooking, maintenance of yard/orchard/pet/vehicles.
- Instructions for running or selling the family business.
- Family video/letters/cassette tapes—for loved ones to find after you are gone.
- Make amends, settle disputes, drop animosities, forgive.
- Relinquish hope for what cannot be—accept yourself as you are!
- Be kind now. Love.

HOMEWORK-11: Edit this list of 'affairs' to custom fit your situation, no matter what your age. Then print it out, and post it in your home. Check off the items already accomplished.

CHOICES AT EIGHTEEN

In the vast arc of a human lifetime, turning 18 is a landmark recognition of legal adulthood, allowing you to vote, enlist, and SIGN YOUR DURABLE POWER OF ATTORNEY FOR HEALTH CARE, aka Advance Directive. (Pick up a copy at the county health department, or your local hospital, and have it notarized. Do it yourself; a lawyer is not necessary.)

You may not drink alcohol until you are 21, but since you are old enough to go to war, you could be adult enough to consider the possibility of a youthful death. Not everyone lives to old age. You all know a peer who has died.

Those who suddenly die while young and healthy, usually allow priceless vital organs to be buried in a grave or lost to cremation. Those vital organs could give back life to somebody else—to somebody's mommy, to someone's lover or beloved son. If killed in an accident, you probably will be transported to a hospital and put on full life support—

machines breathing and pumping blood to keep your organs alive and fresh—until it can be determined you are un-revivable.

Once it is clear you cannot survive, the unbearable wait begins. The medical professionals suffer agonies trying to find a kind way to ask your folks to donate your organs to other patients whose lives could be saved. Then, when asked, your folks feel bludgeoned, violated.

You can be kind to your folks, to those professionals, and possibly to those praying for renewed life, by taking the matter into your own capable hands now: by stipulating in your Durable Power of Attorney for Health Care, whether, or NOT, when you cannot be saved, they may save your organs to help someone else. (Organs must be gleaned as soon as life support stops.) YOU decide. You write it. Matter closed. No further questions have to be asked of anyone else.

Too much responsibility for a youth? Not true, if in elementary school we learned of adult sex practices, had street drugs available to us, had already smoked, or watched our parents divorce while trying to comfort and protect them. If, at age 18, we have been taking the lives of others into our own hands for two years by driving cars, we certainly can have the presence to deliberate, discuss, decide, and to sign that life-giving document. If all 18 year olds signed their own Durable Power of Attorney for Health Care, then 'those other guys who die young' would be covered. And perhaps, after signing it, young adults might be slower to seek dangerous recreation.

> *HOMEWORK-12: Ask a young 18 + person if they would donate organs or not. (Make it easy on yourself—read them this chapter first.)*

KINDNESS

Not many laud kindness these days. Any community is full of kind people. Look at Dale, running a business, active in the Red Cross, launching our farmers' market, feeding any and all stray cats, while raising her three granddaughters, yet she found time to make dinner for her elderly next-door neighbor too. Or Hazel, who for over 20 years was packing meals-on-wheels for people much younger than herself. And Sandy at our local fish market, who followed a customer in sudden pain out to her car, offering to leave the business and drive her home. Marlene, abhorring sickness and hospitals, overcomes her revulsion and visits her old friends weekly, taking mail and reading aloud. Ed at the gas station got down on his back on muddy pavement to check out the car of a frightened (self-service) gas customer and reassure her that her car was safe.

When kindness is totally inconvenient, is when it shines brightest.

You don't have to be a hospice volunteer to care about your neighbor. It takes an astute eye and courage to notice a neighbor in trouble, before you can make yourself available to them.

But, "I don't know what to say," "I don't know how to help them," you protest. Common problem! Mother Theresa gave us the answer:

BE SPECIFIC.

Dale did not get overwhelmed about all the problems of aging— she simply cooked a meal. Hazel did not worry about a menu for 53 people—she simply slipped the sandwich into a baggie, and another, and another, and another. Ed did not struggle with how to find a better car for his frightened customer, he simply untied the hood for her and saw that what she really needed right then was reassurance that the hood would not cause an accident. Sandy did not try to diagnose and treat the woman's pain, simply made sure she could drive and would not be alone.

Reader's Digest once printed an unforgettable story of a man who specifically offered to polish shoes for the funeral after his neighbor died. He could tolerate hearing the widow's tears while he sat silent and absorbed, matching polish to shoe. He only stopped to answer the phone twice, find a Band-Aid for a scraped knee, and turn off the flame under a forgotten whistling teapot. He made no demands, just gave of his presence. By the time they left for the funeral back East, every shoe in that household was clean, with new laces, and the family chaos had been soothed away by his serenity.

BE SPECIFIC

All we really need from each other is someone who genuinely cares. And has skill. There is a way to develop that skill, so that we will not avoid a difficult situation, will not shun those in distress—so that we can defuse a crisis, enable quick decisions, bring calm and comfort—so that each of us can be that caring neighbor. Remembering how you were helped when you were down is the best way.

If not, here is how: you get your own affairs in order, you prepare your own end of life documents, make your own funeral plans, you learn how you might grieve, you face your own natural fears. It might even take some therapy, some healing of your own.

Then, perhaps only then, can you look someone else in the eye, someone who is severely ill, or grieving, or has simply lost their keys—then might you understand them and stand by them.

Getting our affairs in order is a form of self-therapy. And it is free! It is a sure-cure for pathological selfishness. It and your life-experiences, your own personal healed sorrows, are good preparation towards being randomly kind to others. Amazingly kind.

> **HOMEWORK-13: Study your own list of 'affairs' to put in order. Then start with the easiest one first … just one.**

Chapter 6

NEWS ABOUT DEATH
"It's Better Than the Alternative"

Now, there are three dying options:

1) you die, soon;
2) you grow old and die;
3) you grow old and don't die. Just grow older and older, more tattered and worn out, more uncomfortable and older and older. And older.

Much of my counseling work has been about #3, about all the problems around people getting older and older, and not getting dead. People will keep going until their loved ones relent and excuse them, somehow agreeing that it is no longer worth it to stay in a pain-ridden, useless body. We need to understand that our doctors are bound by their philosophy and ethics to keep us alive as long as possible, even longer than they themselves would want to be kept alive. Often, as long as we are surrounded by folks who are invested in keeping us alive, we seem to be stuck in our cracked shells.

We know how and when to die. Without employing any artificial method, we have the power to slip out naturally when we are ready.

Please let us notice this.

We all know someone who slipped away well, who seemed to wait only until the family had gathered—maybe during the holidays. Did he perhaps glean energy from all those convened, energy to aid him, to empower his launch out of here? Or did she want folks to be together to comfort one another and further bond while big transitions happened in the family? Or was she waiting until everyone else had 'ripened,' had let go, before she left?

You have also seen the one who hung on and on and on. "He's such a fighter," you say. I tend to believe that he had to fight his inclination to go. He had to stay alive until YOU got good and ready for him to leave. If you haven't forgiven him nor he you, he'll stick around, waiting for the chain to break, for you to give him permission somehow, in word or gesture, to let go.

My intention is to stay alert to my choices—to my personal freedom. My doctor will keep me alive physically, as long as he perceives I am not ready to die. And that is exactly how he takes it, as long as I accept his life-prolonging offerings.

So, why are we living into our dependency? Because we choose to. Because we accept the products of the business of medicine unquestioningly. I am grateful for the medical care I have freely accepted over the years. And henceforth, I intend to look at those choices and make them more consciously and keep them in tune with what I really want.

When you say, "Oh, I want to die in my sleep," or "I just hope a big Mack truck ..." I perceive those clichés as extremely ostrich.

Why not say, instead, "When I get pneumonia, do not treat it." Or, "If I do not have sense enough to eat, for God's sake, do not feed me." Or, "No more tests, Doc. Just keep me at home with palliative care. Give me a kind hospice nurse, morphine, and let me enjoy the view out my window and the dog at my feet until I just snooze off and never wake up." Now, that IS do-able.

Not to mention the ethics of allowing those mega-insurance-bucks which statistically are squandered on the ONE last hopeless year of desperately grabbing at life. Why not refuse those transplanted organs which younger people need? Why not refuse to consign thousands of insurance dollars for open-heart surgery at 85? Or decline to be fed for years while in an irreversible coma? I am appalled at the waste that people allow on themselves.

No, it should never be written into the law that we be denied medical treatment. And the law allows us to refuse medical treatment. But we need to make it socially acceptable to refuse medical treatment, even if it means shortening the lifespan. In other words, if your dad said he wanted no more doctoring, no more hospitals, then no one could judge you as being neglectful of him when you kept him home and he died quickly. Humanitarian physicians would be so very relieved.

Me? Given the rate at which my bones and memory are disintegrating, it is my intention not to live more than another 20 years. With my durable power of attorney for health care in place, and my good friends in agreement, I expect to be refusing aggressive medical treatment as the need arises. In my 60's, no organ transplants, no dialysis, no cancer treatment if there is less than a 55 percent chance of cure. In my 70's, no open-heart surgery, either. In my 80's, no treatment whatsoever, other than palliative. Sounds glib? You are right. But, in spite of what they say about the road to hell, good intentions are better than none at all.

LYLE

A native of New Orleans, Lyle stuck around for Mardi Gras. She had imported a smashing Mardi Gras party to her new California hometown just the year before. At her second annual· Mardi Gras dance, one week before her death, she was filmed singing at the microphone, in a long, wild wig, playing maracas, and inciting the crowd to keep dancing and celebrating. Then she was nearly done.

A young, gallant woman, from her pillow bald Lyle could admire her opposite wall adorned with the flowered and feathered floppy hats, beanies, skull caps, sailor's hat, witches peak, and velvet berets that once enveloped gobs of her hair. Her parents sat at the foot of her bed, below the hats. Lyle's little boys had been living with them while she was waging war on her breast cancer. Her fragmented family had just returned from Florida, but not because she was victorious.

Single breasted, breathing heavily since cancer now filled her lungs as well, she was finally calling a truce.

"I'm sorry. I just can't fight any more," she confessed to her little sons, one lying on each side of her. "I'm not going to do any more treatments, and I will be dying soon." After a thick silence, I asked Lyle,

"What's to become of your boys?"

She looked one deeply in his eyes, then rolled her head on her pillow and gazed into her other son's eyes. Then she pronounced categorically:

"They are going to be … just … FINE." And all three nodded.

Then she was done.

And they left for Florida.

And Lyle stayed in that bed. She stopped gazing at the hats, slept on and off and died quietly a few days later.*

IN-LAW

"Well, what IS holding him back?" I asked one man's daughter-in-law, outside the front gate as I was leaving.

"Sometimes an in-law will have more objective insights on the family," I encouraged her. They were all exhausted, taking shifts to care for dad, and he was living in extreme discomfort, lasting way past the expectations of his healthcare workers.

She glanced at her husband who was leaning on the gate, toeing the gravel at his feet. He nodded to her.

"Yes, there is one thing and they don't talk about it. Unresolved …" she explained, "their foster brother. He's estranged from the family, has even threatened his brothers' mother. No one trusts him. But Pops is so worried about him. "

"I'll bet your Pops hangs on until that is resolved," I challenged her husband.

"I'm willing, but there is no resolution."

"How about this? You brothers gather with dad, telling him you will always protect mom, and that however you can help your stepbrother, you will make every effort to do so. Is that possible?"

They did just that. Although not actually a resolution, their heart-to-heart with dad gave him the peace of mind to be able to let go that night. It seemed clear to his sons that it was all he was waiting for.

*See Bob Markee's Blue Raven Productions video documentary, aired in 1995 on PBS stations across the nation: "A Friend Called Lyle."

BOB AND THE "ANGEL"

Bob drove an old white pickup when he came to me for counseling, had rented a nice house among shading oak trees, always wore fitted Levis and white sneakers. I saw his sick partner, weak and bony under a bed-sheet, only on the night of his death. He was dying of AIDS. The hospice nurses had explained to me that none of the opportunistic diseases had gotten him. He had endured them all. Mike was actually dying of AIDS itself, of the deterioration of the brain stem, so that seizures would get worse and worse and finally one would take him.

The horrendous, spitting-gargoyle seizures were coming hourly, and Bob couldn't stand to watch them alone any more. So I went over to spend the night there, to keep vigil with him. We sat up, on either side of the hospital bed in the living room. I had counseled him to give permission to let go, which he had done. With each seizure he'd repeat a romantic little phrase:

"It's OK. Just let the angel of death take you, Sweetie."

Between his seizures, I had time to ponder. Why was this man taking so long to die? What was he waiting for? Bob and I stood over him on either side of the hospital bed, holding his flailing arms down during another gruesome seizure, then we resumed our bedside seats and, across the still form of the man in the coma, knowing he could hear us, I asked Bob, "You guys have been monogamous for decades, so how did Mike get AIDS?"

"He slipped once, went up to San Francisco to the bath houses, got it there, then he never strayed again. We didn't know he had AIDS for years."

"Did you forgive him?"

"Yes, I did ... guess I never told him so."

This simple confession and absolution was for both of them. And Bob seemed somehow relieved. With the next seizure, there was no simpering.

"Forgodssake, JUST... LET... GO!" Bob cried. Mike exhaled at the seizure's finish, then never took another breath.

Yes, I keep finding that life and death IS in our hands, in our will to live or die. (Or God's will, however your beliefs express it. After 21 years of witnessing deaths, I believe that, in determining the moment of our death, our will is in cahoots with God's.) Let us notice that the moment of leaving seems clearly chosen by us, and stop whining about euthanasia, or about the unpleasantness of dwelling in a nursing home. Let's do our homework and just get our act together.

> *HOMEWORK-14: Discuss with your closest family/ friends whether each wants cremation or burial. Write it down, date and file it with Vital Documents list.*

Chapter 7

EUTHANASIA?
"We Don't Need It"

"What about euthanasia?" people often ask me.

"We don't need it!" is always my clear response, based on years of sitting with people as they died naturally. Here's why:

The concept of euthanasia supposedly is that a person is ready to die, and killing them artificially eliminates their suffering, or eliminates their dependency on the care of others, eliminates the family inconveniences and expenditures, and eliminates a long drawn-out illness in the family. On the surface, it sounds reasonable.

But anyone who has witnessed the best of hospice, knows that actually euthanasia would eliminate their own letting go, would rob their 'free will' to die when they are ready.

WE ALREADY KNOW HOW TO DIE.

ONCE WE ARE READY TO DIE, WE DIE ALL ON OUR OWN.

So why shorten the length of illness by killing, when the patient himself can shorten it naturally by refusing life-prolonging treatment, by refusing food and medicine?

Ready? We die naturally in a matter of days, when we are fully ready. If we are not dead yet, we are not ready yet, and so euthanasia can only cause premature death.

Waiting? If we say we are ready, or appear to be ready, but are still alive, then we are in a waiting mode. If we can figure out what we are waiting for (that's the goal of hospice counseling), we can deal with it, and then release.

Suffering? To eliminate suffering we want to kill our dying people. But good palliative care minimizes suffering, enables the getting ready while easing the symptoms of the wise body's natural shut-down process.

The proponents of euthanasia are totally overlooking that:

- hospice palliative medicine allows you to die without suffering, naturally, and of your own free will,
- hospice counseling helps you get ready more quickly,
- euthanasia only interferes with the natural resolution to a lifetime.

Sudden accidental death is trickier, but not so different. But with time and foreknowledge of a terminal condition, if left to our own devices, our 'own free will' picks the precise moment of leaving. Based on what? That is a mystery one can't tamper with. Partly, however, it seems like we wait until we glean an inkling that those we care about are going to be okay without us, and then we cut loose.

Mostly we wait until we are sure our life-partner, or our offspring, will have purpose after we are gone. As long as s/he lives only to care for us, we are responsible for fulfilling his/her need to be needed, and so we stick around for her/him.

"Waiting for permission to go," is one way of saying it. But the permission doesn't lie in the words of the family members as much as in their conviction that they will be able to survive without that departed person. Some people wait until she resumes attending her women's club meetings again, or until he starts playing golf again.

Even though her body is too sick to live—way beyond being inhabitable—if that loving young mother hasn't yet figured out how her children are going to be kept safe, she won't die. In this case, artificially and prematurely causing her death would be destructive. (As it is in every case.) When she is ready to relinquish her jobs, that mother will be gone very quickly, all on her own. (As will each of us.)

Lyle could say her kids would be OK, because she admonished them to be so with her eyes, affirming she had faith in their inner fiber to make it, thereby gifting them with faith in themselves. And she trusted her parents to protect them.

When the care-giving spouse begins to show interest in other members of the family, or in quilting or fishing or club work—some sign of willingness to survive in the involvement with others—only then can the sick partner let go.

My sense is that when people are genuinely ready to go, nothing here interests them any more; they have literally turned to face a different horizon. And then, euthanasia is unnecessary. When someone protests that he wants out of here, and needs euthanasia (or suicide), you can listen to all his reasons for wanting to go and agree that it seems time to go. Then you ask him why is he still here? What is the hook that is keeping him here? The itch? What is he still waiting for from this life? If life is just too painful, too disappointing, too hard—that means he still wants or aspires or hopes. And THAT means he is not yet finished, not resolved.

A little review of his life—balancing the present disappointments with previous successes—might just do the trick. Or encouraging the bickering children to make peace and take turns caring for the dying parent, which indicates the ability to stand by each other in the future. Intimate and unpleasant care-giving of a dying parent is a GREAT crash course, a finishing school for the aspiring next generation. As soon as they show signs of growing up, the patient easily slips away.

And so, if we request euthanasia because we are not dead yet, which actually means not quite ready yet, then that is violence—violence to our family's, and to our own, psycho/social/spiritual evolvement.

Of course, there are the other fine reasons for opposing euthanasia, as well! There's the political danger of legalizing the riddance of the physically useless people of society, (while wasting their social, cultural, or spiritual worth). It is too easy a progression from euthanizing someone who 'needs' and asks for it, through euthanizing someone who 'needs' and hasn't enough sense to ask for it, to euthanizing someone whose need does not matter as much as their economic liability to society.

But these reasons are trivial compared to the overriding FACT: We do not need assistance to die when we are ready to die, simply because we die all on our own when we are ready to die.

So, if YOU are asking for euthanasia, please talk with your hospice counselor who can help you figure out why you are not yet dead all on your very own.

Or else, here are some convincing examples of our need to determine our own dying:

THE MODEL

Rachel had been a model who married well. Her girlfriends in our town were her manicurists, massage therapists, hairdressers, who stood by her. I visited her at home during her illness. The last time I saw her, she was in the hospital, perched like a monkey on the top end of her raised hospital bed, bony legs all folded up in front of her, knees at neck, her hair in rollers, her 20 nails all works of art. Gripping a hand mirror, she was painting her eyes, gorgeous luminous eyes.

"Getting ready," she declared.

And later that night, she died made up and combed to look her very best, as only she knew how to do.

MINA

Mina, retired RN, was one savvy old gal. She understood things that woman's wisdom and years of caring for others had allowed her to see. Then my hospice volunteer, Mina was sitting with a dying old woman who didn't talk much, but within their single-phrased dialogue, she heard,

"I can't go yet. My kitchen floor is dirty."

Now, I might have taken that as some sort of a metaphor for 'unfinished business.' But Mina sensed it WAS the unfinished business. She got out the mop and bucket, and scrubbed that kitchen floor. Watching from her living room sofa, the patient waited until Mina sat down again, then sighed deeply and thanked her. And within a few hours she died.

BILLY

Billy and his mom were scared when she phoned me. Stumpy Billy, gloomy and hesitant, led me to his mother's bedroom. Like Mae West and pushing 80, mom's hair was peroxide blond and wrapped around her head, and she draped herself diagonally across her bedcover wearing a black lace slip.

"I called you because we both have bad heart problems. I have taken care of Billy all his life, and now he takes care of me.

What will happen when one of us dies? It could happen any time now."

I learned that Billy had been taken out of school as a kid when he started having rages. They thought he was retarded. I determined that he might be only learning-disabled, that the rages came from the frustration of his struggles in school and the oppression of his lifestyle under the tyranny of his mother. I consulted with an angel of a counselor in the local college's Disabled Students' Center. We conspired to get Billy traveling to campus on the bus, taking a few introductory classes for managing life with a disability. The man was ecstatic. He was having a life—after 50 years of no life, he was having a real life.

Soon thereafter, relieved about her son, Mom did indeed die. Under excellent guidance, Billy got an apartment near campus and finished his first year of college. He had triumphed, and so he was ready, too. Billy died proud.

HOMEWORK-15: Recall your own best experience with a good death. Or get a few friends together to share.

Chapter 8

DYING
"How Does It Work?"

Because we've watched too much TV, we equate dying with trauma. Most dying need not be traumatic. A good death is not traumatic. Death in the natural course of a lifetime, long or short—and especially with the help of hospice—need not be traumatic.

There are many ways for a lifetime to end. The natural way, through old age or illness, has the advantage of allowing us some time to prepare. The drawback, however, is that once we know we are dying, we become a sort of pariah because people think of us, and treat us, differently. That isolation can make us very lonely.

OUTCAST

Notice what could happen to me with a 'terminal' illness. My doctor tells me that tests indicate that my illness will cause my death. With that, I am made to feel somehow lacking, a failure, an outcast. I might encounter social pitfalls after receiving scary test results from a physician—which will make me instinctively want to keep it a secret. Here are some examples.

- Everything becomes hazy, confusing to me (I'm in shock).
- I lose my jobs, all of them (lover, parent, executive, co-worker).
- People shun me.
- People talk over my head, about me, deciding things for me.
- People are secretive.

- People fake cheerfulness, hold back tears.
- They put up a wall of diplomacy, implying that it is not nice to die.
- People protect me from my own death!
- I am pressured to spend thousands of dollars to patch up, to poison, to force feed, to keep operating this diseased, weakened, pain-ridden, worn-out body.
- I must make horrendous decisions (with scanty information) that I am too traumatized to make.
- People put me in a scary, sterile, noisy, over-lit, unfamiliar environment, just when I need my own bed.
- Solicitous relatives appear from nowhere.
- Families haggle over my belongings. Or they discount me when I try to distribute my belongings.
- Later, people try to prolong my dying by forced feeding.
- My spouse tells me lies, my doctor mumbles or advises with technical medical language.
- If I stay home, my doctor never comes, hardly returns calls.
- My spouse is scared and doesn't know what to do.
- There is much spousal and family bickering.
- Chaos, anxiety and panic, as well as illness and care-giving, freeze my household's normal workings.
- Most people stay away.

REMEDY

That good friend, like a hospice volunteer, can ease that isolation a) by aligning with the dying person as his advocate, and b) by enabling the family members to understand how things are from the dying person's point of view, such as:

1. Dying is not a family project, nor a marital project.
   - Dying is a solo job.
   - The spouse can comfort the patient, grieve with the patient, but cannot do the prep work or the dying for the patient.

- "We're in this thing together" is not an accurate concept. ("I'm right here with you," or "I'm standing by you (your need to live on or to die now), whichever you need to do," might be more encouraging.)
- The patient is alone with his/her project.
- The dying one needs to be understood, respected, allowed.

2. When you die suddenly, your roles die WITH you. When you die slowly, your roles die AHEAD of you.
   - You lose power over others, to protect them or rule them.
   - You have a new sense of inadequacy, or failure, or shame, or disgust at self and body.
   - You suffer embarrassment when being cared for by anyone else, especially personal care by son or daughter or spouse.
   - You strategize and power play, trying to maintain some control over your life; you become a tyrant in bed.
   - You have morphed from head of household to difficult, needy patient.
   - Maybe without admitting it, you feel betrayed by loved ones simply because they will continue on in life. Jealousy!

3. Dying is hard work.
   - The energy spent promoting life in the body must be redirected towards launching out of the body.
   - Your life needs to be sorted out: its contributions, its regrets, forgiveness—at least unconsciously. It's more helpful if you can do a debriefing, a wrap-up, to feel complete or done, in order to let go—by reviewing your whole life.
   - You try to protect family members: to save them discomfort during your dying.
   - You watch and protect and prepare your loved ones towards their loss of you.
   - You handle material arrangements yourself, or assigning them, when really too sick to tolerate the jobs, i.e. finances, legalities, child-care, sale of business or of extra vehicles, transference of assets, etc.
   - Pain is hard labor—braving through it is exhausting—both physical and emotional pain.

- Bowel problems and body smells happen just when people want to visit.
- You are laboring to release the natural will to live, relinquishing interest in life, which alarms the very loved ones you want to protect.
- Without full faculties you must gather your wits for judgment calls. (When is it not worth the medical treatment?) (Whom to trust?) (When is it not worth pain/discomfort/dependence to stay alive?) (Have my loved ones come around yet? Will they be OK if I go now?)
- You learn to disassociate from your own sick body, to tolerate living in it, and to prepare to launch.
- You are gradually withdrawing from loved ones—days or weeks before death—ignoring their dismay.
- You experience the other side as well as this side, with subsequent disorientation, mentioning persons of one side to those of the other, or addressing them both from the same state of awareness (talking about deceased loved ones in the present tense).

4. I, the valuable neighbor, pal, or in-law, need to remember that the dying person is working too hard to have time for:
   - My agenda for him
   - My need to be appreciated
   - My own religious beliefs
   - My food
   - My cheer
   - My outside big world news

5. The dying person accepts as companion someone who clicks—often identified by a meaningful word or a moment's eye contact:
   - Who leaves his/her own needs and defenses outside.
   - Who can touch and hold a hand, or sit very near without touch or voice.
   - Who can look the patient in the eye with utter self-honesty, silence, understanding.
   - Who can honor the patient's pace, beliefs and needs.

- Who can hear when the patient refers to death, either directly or metaphorically, and can follow the cue and respond in kind, speaking the same language.
- Who is matter of fact, can ignore the body's condition, and can treat the patient like the whole person he is, with respect, humor, total sincerity, ease, no drama, no pity, and with simple brotherly/sisterly interest and compassion.

(Note: Experience and dying patients' instincts have sometimes shown that an in-law comes best equipped to provide this necessary alliance.)

GEORGE & BERNICE

George died a good death, with the luxury of being among people who remembered until his very last breath that he was George. George was my prized example of human mastery.

I would sit with George while his wife, Bernice, of a long, loyal marriage and two grown daughters, would go out on errands. He was no longer eating much, but, lying sunken in the hospital bed in the center of their apartment living room, he would ask me to dig out the stashed box of chocolates. We would each have a piece, savoring it and snickering like culprits. George and Bernice were both frank about his imminent death, no secrets, no further need to talk about it. He was admirably unalarmed about the whole prospect.

"Are you ready? Anything left undone?" I asked George one day after the chocolate caper.

"Yes," he whispered feebly, "My best friend since elementary school. I haven't seen him for years. I want to say goodbye."

"Is now a good time?" I asked, ready to search out phone numbers. George pointed to the desk. I called his friend who answered the phone. I explained who and where I was. "How is George doing?" he asked.

"Oh, he's doing great! He's extremely weak physically, and speaks in whispers, so to save his breath, let me fill you in a bit. He'll be dying soon, and he's quite comfortable here, in a hospital bed in the living room. He's hearing what I say to you, so you need to just talk to him and not expect many words back."

They talked for many minutes. George was clearly satisfied with that conversation.

The next day, I found him surrounded by a bevy of women—hospice nurse, home-health aide, Bernice, and me. We were all joking around his bed, teasing him but not requiring much back from him except his emaciated grin, which goaded us on.

"Be nice to know when you're going, George, so we can be here with Bernice."

"I'll be taking the red-eye." The others laughed knowingly.

"What's the red-eye?" asked I, the ignorant California girl.

They stopped their banter to explain that, back East in their days, this was the train that departed nightly at two in the morning.

"Oh, George," I asked, "are you dying tonight at 2 am?"

"Nope, tomorrow," he responded.

Bernice wouldn't let us come back the next evening. She wanted time alone with him, and if that was when he left, well, it would be okay.

Sure enough, the next night at 2 am, George died, with Bernice holding his hand. She was high for days, in bliss, one might say. George's wasn't just a tidy death. It was a tidy, small, simple, blessed event. We were all grateful to know him and witness that, to know that we too, could die well. It doesn't take much ....

Bernice's tears flowed copiously in the months thereafter as she accustomed herself to never seeing him again, while gloating about his excellence in dying.

Did George need euthanasia?

HOW TO BE WITH A FRIEND WHEN DEATH IS NEAR

During the natural dying process, your friend will slowly withdraw from interest in this life, from food, from talk, from you. This is normal. And it helps if you support this process. Let it be. Forget your needs to be validated, accepted, and important. Tune in to what your friend needs. Your presence will be welcome only if you need NOTHING from your friend.

You are important, and can be of great help. Have courage and trust your own instincts to show you how to be there.

Help in the physical care as needed, or step away while it is given by others.

Bring beauty, warmth, and life into the room with favorite music, poetry, news, flowers from the garden, a blossom tied to the bedrail, a pet, a child, colorful bedclothes, a big grin.

Always focus on the person you know to be in there, not on the externals of body appearance, smells and sounds, monitors, IVs, oxygen tank—which can be frightening and worrisome. Relate directly to your friend, ignoring all those distractions.

Sit at same eye-level as the patient – never above. This is crucial, even if it means perching on a stool or the floor. Keeping your head lower than the patient's reminds you that you are not superior, not in charge—that this is HIS show.

Speak gently, clearly and simply. Address the patient directly— only speak to others in the room if you are clearly including the patient in the conversation. Look into the eyes of the one who is ill. Even if the eyes are closed or glazed, assume you are being heard.

Touch and be close. Or notice if patient needs his space. Share your tears and the feelings that seem unacceptable. It opens intimacy, breaks down the isolation of the patient, his loneliness.

Talk about the lifetime of the patient, with him and/or with others at the bedside. Even if the patient is comatose, it helps to have family in the room poring over photos, or watching family movies. Get them involved in an oral review of the patient's life, and when possible, get the patient to tell his/her own life story, or bits of it.

Say what you need to say, to make peace in the relationship. That might mean forgiveness, apology, appreciation, the greater meaning of your relationship. Share the specific things you remember—the playful, the inspiring, and the ordinary. Until the moment of death, there is only life, and in life, there is always humor.

Go easy on yourself if you do something that is not as helpful as you had hoped. It is difficult to know what to do in this strange and alien time.

Sit silently. Assume your silent presence at the bedside is perceived as comforting. You can silently pray or meditate there. Or rest. And breathe.

IRIS

Iris paused in her pacing, an Asian-American woman, brilliant, educated, tough and muscled from running and tennis. The winter sun cut through high condo windows, striking her fingers fiddling at her kitchen counter. Then she paced again, while I became infected with her helplessness.

Tight-lipped, Iris seethed and hissed of her marriage to Charles, an older man who promised to stay with her the rest of her life. Now he'd had a massive stroke, perhaps was dying, and stuck in the nearby costly convalescent hospital. Her fury at that betrayal kept her pacing, not knowing what to do. Frantic creature, she was inconsolable, steely and dry-eyed with rage. She couldn't afford to keep him for long in the nursing home, and she certainly was "not the Florence Nightingale type." So she would pace her hillside house and avoid visiting the man who no longer could speak to her and guide her.

After some weeks, and much counseling, I managed to get some friends, the Beckers, to meet Iris at the hospital, to help make a visit easier.

We gathered at the foot of Charles' bed, and Iris stayed with her back against the wall, as far from him as possible. I asked for some history. The Beckers explained they met Iris at church, and Mr. Becker had become her bridge partner.

"Weren't you jealous of this guy, Charles?" I asked the unresponsive man in the bed with closed eyes. He didn't respond, but I kept addressing him with teasing every once in a while, to keep reminding Iris that her husband was indeed present with us, 'semi-comatose' or not.

I asked her how they first met. Both engineers, they had met at work. Her tears finally brimmed, recounting their first date, as she moaned, "It was love at first sight."

"Love at first sight, eh, Charles? Wow, you must be some guy!" My lighthearted banter gently evoked a review of their life together, he being her mentor and refuge. Sensing that she had finally forgiven Charles and come to terms with his leaving, we outsiders drifted off, leaving her alone with her husband, for the first time since his stroke.

She drew up a seat to the head of his bed. Leaning over, she put her hand on his covered shoulder.

"I don't know what I'm going to do without you," she

whispered to her closest friend and confidant. That lament implied that she knew he was dying, and was willing to survive him.

He turned his head slightly to her as if to whisper a secret in her ear, and exhaled his last breath.

> *HOMEWORK-16: Plan your own disposition. There are four steps to said planning. If you have already accomplished some, your assignment is merely to complete the next step.*
> - *First Step: Discuss your choices with your loved ones: burial vs. cremation, site of gathering, site of disposition, preferred funeral home, etc.*
> - *Second Step: Write down your choices, date and file this with Vital Documents.*
> - *Third Step: Pre-plan and register your disposition with your chosen funeral home.*
> - *Fourth Step: Pay for it.*

Chapter 9

GOOD GRIEF!
"Avoiding Work?"

GRIEFWORK—A JOB TO BE DONE

Why call it griefwork? There are heavy-duty tasks to be accomplished before a person can survive the loss of a beloved intimate. Grief work requires mega amounts of emotional energy, leaving you exhausted, so brain-tired you can't think straight. The newly bereaved cannot remember, sort, prioritize, choose, cognate, train competently for a new career, nor show good judgment.

This exhaustion is GOOD reason for making NO major life decisions (to sell the house, remarry, start a new business, return to college, apply for a job) until grieving is done.

And if you do grieve, it will be done. And you will feel like yourself again. It is like 'doing time.' You cannot shorten it. Just ride it out—the moods, waves of anger or longing or weeping, absent-mindedness. And then one day you will notice you are lighter and freer and smarter than you have been for many months.

Grieving people are chronically tired people. Mourning means fatigue. Are they lazy, self-indulgent, just feeling sorry for themselves?

NO. Sitting on the sofa, staring into space, contemplating the enormity of their changed life, is HARD LABOR. Although they are neither sweating nor producing anything, they are working internally to accommodate this change, to figure out how to survive it and emerge with fresh new energy, new peace of mind, new interest in their world.

This is a big job, folks. It takes time! Not a week. More like a year. They deserve some slack, some credit, praise, and understanding. Help them with the routine chores which temporarily overwhelm them, and allow all the down-time they need to accomplish that crucial big job of surviving in an alien new world.

Too bad we did away with 'widow's weeds.' Wearing black was useful. It used to be a signal that read,

"I am in mourning. Forgive me if I don't join in. Please don't make any demands on me. I am temporarily unsociable and unpleasant. Just to get up in the morning, and figure out who I am and how I am to live occupies me, and I cannot attend to anyone else's needs until my 'homework' is done. So please stand back and stand by and stay loyal."

FIGHT OR FLIGHT

The thirsting wild creature approaches the mountain stream and begins to drink. She lifts her head at the sound of the enemy approaching. Sniffing the scents on the breeze, she prepares for the enemy's attack. How does she prepare?

Fight-or-flight reflex takes over the normal functioning of her body. Extra adrenaline is released for emergency energy, and her heart beats faster to distribute the adrenaline. And more oxygen. Hair stands on end to appear bigger, fear-scent issues from glands in her open mouth, hackles go up, teeth bare while growling—all to scare her enemy. Bowel and bladder evacuate, so she can move faster. Sleep, appetite, thirst are depressed so she will not be distracted by grazing and can remain wary. She is in emergency mode, ready to run like the wind or fight to the death.

Human bodies have the same programmed responses. Since we are social animals and cannot survive without the tribe, our enemy is death or a life-threatening diagnosis in the family. When frightened, we wet our pants and our hairless body gets goose-bumps. We enter that strange altered state of mind caused by extra adrenaline. In that crisis mode we fidget, cannot concentrate or finish anything. We become vigilant and cannot sleep, nor eat, nor pay bills, nor drive well. We cannot manage taxes, the kids, shopping, or the job. We are not at our best in anything we do. But fight-or-flight reflex is temporary. With time and safety, it subsides. So, at first, the relatives gather to guide us, while the neighborhood casserole brigade feeds us.

And not until we cry or laugh or sweat or bellow or exercise sufficiently for the excess adrenaline to be released—can we begin to get back to normal.

Meanwhile, no amount of chiding by our well-functioning fellows is going to reverse or hasten that natural, biological, mind-numbing response to tragedy.

While we are in shock—yes, it is the same shock that keeps us from feeling our wounds after being injured in a car accident—that shock, or natural anesthetic, protects us from an anguish so intense we could not survive it.

That natural shock state might bore others, but it is quite valuable to the bereaved. It keeps us alive until we can tolerate the loss, until we can acclimate ourselves to the new environment without that precious person in it. Shock is our haven. So is denial.

PHASES OF GRIEF

Like the ingredients of a salad, the phases of grieving are tossed together and you never know what will come up on your hapless fork: numbness, regrouping, emotion, inner recovery, social recovery, altruism.

The first ingredient of grieving is numbness. Your job, while naturally anesthetized, is to do all the busy work of mourning: the gathering of kinfolk, the announcement of your loss, accepting condolences and assistance while you bury him, clear out his closet, and begin to let go of his physical presence in your house. Any of those tangible activities enables you to come out of this numbness of shock, and accept the loss as real.

Then emotion. When the anesthetic wears off, sometimes weeks or months later, you FEEL it. Sadness, loss, anger, guilt, howling anguish, such longing! Pain. You (and your dismayed family) think you are falling apart. But it is actually a sign of progress—this ability to tolerate the emotions. You might need to talk, cry, rage, wail, fight, flail, pace, fidget, labor and sweat, shout, belly-laugh, then weep some more. The power of these passions is just too overwhelming, so you return to numbness for another time-out, and go to work or to sleep, or watch a funny movie.

Once you have released some emotional pain, sloughed off excess adrenaline, you might find yourself sitting quietly, staring into space, lost in thought, regrouping. In your solitude, you wonder why he went first, who you are, what good you are now, and why were you left 'holding the bag' called life? This true sadness seems to mimic depression. But it is actually healthy, productive, healing, time well spent.

Inner recovery is another ingredient. When you develop a new inner sense of yourself, discovering new abilities (writing your first check or washing your first load of clothes becomes a triumph), new perspectives on life, new spiritual muscles, new self-confidence, new faith.

You'll begin to notice social recovery as well. The energy for externally dealing with people is back—to return to church, go to a potluck, or enjoy a concert.

The last ingredient will be altruism. Not false altruism as an avoidance mechanism—the addiction of fixing others to avoid your own pain—but the genuine renewal of energy where you not only tolerate others again, you actually find new, deeper compassion for them, and satisfaction in helping (comforting a bereaved neighbor, encouraging your grandchild, serving food to the needy). You feel the kinship, that you are no longer alone.

So, these phases—the numbness, the raw emotions, the quiet despondence, the social recovery, the new confidence, the kindness for others—are tossed like a salad. You jump unpredictably from phase to phase and back again—helping today, crying later, then numb again. One of the hundreds of bereaved who have come for counseling said, "It is like walking through a mine-field on a sunny day. You feel pretty good, sky is clear, and, suddenly—BOOM!—you are devastated again."

Bereavement is a nasty, mean price to pay for becoming a new, improved human being. But it is worth it! People broken with sorrow can mend, strengthen, deepen their compassion, find merriment and fresh new life.

Bereavement is the opportunity to do some needed remodeling on yourself. You certainly do not want to hear that while you are grieving.

But what grace when you look back and notice it later.

AVOID VS. ACCOMPLISH

"How long will it take me to get over this?" they moan, when they finally get up their nerve to come to my office for bereavement counseling.

"As long as it takes you to go through it," I reply. "How you are progressing?"

Grieving is hard work. And, as with any other huge job, we like to avoid it. When you are alone, pensive, blue, miserable, or in outright anguish, you are getting the job done. When you are feeling better, that is when you are resting from the job.

Most pain—cancer pain, toothache, headache—is to be stopped. On the contrary, the pain of sorrow is to be encouraged in that first year, for it is the activity of healing.

However, we have a multitude of ways to avoid that healing: Stay drunk. Oversleep. Street drugs. World travel. House-moving. Day-long TV. Immediate new sex partners. Overworking. Compulsively shopping. Zealously fixing other people's problems. (Here you could insert your own personal avoidance technique—otherwise known as "addiction").

People always admonish bereaved friends to 'stay busy.' Right, staying busy is a distraction from your grief, a rest from the work. Often you need the rest. But it is not getting the job done. Workaholism can be the surest sign of unhealed pain in your life that you cannot face.

The healthy tasks of mourning, on the other hand, are all the appropriate jobs facing the bereaved which are so painful that kinfolk mistakenly want to do them for you. Don't let them. Do your own mourning.

Any of these tasks of mourning help us work out of shock and back into clarity of mind:

hearing the "terminal" diagnosis
being informed of the death,
witnessing the death,
announcing the death,
planning the service,
attending the service,
strewing the ashes,

ordering the marker,

changing names on legal documents,

disposing of clothes and belongings,

writing to relatives,

writing and re-reading the obituary,

visiting and re-visiting the graveside,

rearranging house to suit the survivors,

going to places you used to attend together, and especially,

talking about your loved one,

telling stories about your life together.

Do as many of these as are available to you (with assistance, of course, of good, silent, comforting company). In time—perhaps a year, maybe more—your grief will be healing nicely.

> HOMEWORK-17: *Make a list of the tasks of mourning that you personally have accomplished when bereaved, even if only about your demolished car.*

TEARS

Nature invented tears. Tears are everyone's natural cleansers, natural medicine, natural healers. How? Whenever we get alarmed, our body pumps extra adrenaline to keep us strong and functioning. Once it's no longer needed, tears almost seem to wash that extra adrenaline out of us. Ever notice how shaky and tense you were before crying, and how spent and limp afterwards? Doctors know that crying is somehow good for the brain, reduces mental stress.

Do not say, "I broke down," "I fell apart." Think, rather, "I had a good cry. I released pain. It can't stay in ME and fester. I am quieted. Somber and still, I feel relieved. I can take a deep breath. This is good."

I wish I could get paid what Ingrid Bergman got for crying on screen. So beautiful and devout, eyes uplifted, delicate row of teardrops down her cheek. Not me. I'm a problem crier. My face grimaces like a gargoyle. Not only do tears flow, but I am embarrassed by drooling mouth and dripping nose. No, crying is not supposed to be a pretty thing. Yet I am so happy to see you cry. As a bereavement counselor, I am gratified to see your tears, your healing tears.

I once heard that the Latin concept of "macho" came from the Greeks. Real Greek men had the power of their passions. Passion in war, passion in love, passion in grief. Crying and wailing in the throes of pain and grief was an attribute of men, of warriors. Somehow the Anglo cults of John Wayne and Clint Eastwood turned that around, so that the stiff upper lip, the retention of grief, became the model for our masculine. Thank goodness for the tears of Tom Cruise, Danny Glover, and "Good Will Hunting" nowadays. Let me tell you, in my office, I have seen the healthiest and most masculine of grown men cry. I have seen it, over and over. Crying heals.

You do not have a bottomless well of tears. If you cry them out, they will dry up. And you will feel a release, a relief. I promise. Not allowing tears to flow naturally can be a discredit to nature and a disservice to yourself.

Those who simply cannot cry have alternatives. Do not hold it in— sweat it out, shout it out, labor it out, play it out, sing it out, laugh it out, but GET IT OUT!

Chapter 10

HOLIDAYS AND GRIEF
"Goodbye, Norman Rockwell"

HOLIDAY BEREAVEMENT

How she dreads the holidays without him here! Your newly widowed mom or aunt or grandma finds it so very difficult to get through the holiday season—not only because she misses the partner she had for fifty Thanksgivings, but because of fatigue. Emotional/ spiritual/social fatigue is caused by such a major loss. Even body fatigue daunts her, causing a temporarily muddled brain. The energy spent to survive in a world without him just wipes her out. And since family gatherings are usually heralded, hosted, ushered, and served by the most mature woman of the family—when widowed, she can be OVERWHELMED.

Yes, you say, you are grieving too. But not like she is. Her whole lifestyle, her daily routine, what she gets up for, is shattered. If your daily life has remained basically unaltered by his death, you have no idea.

Mom cannot dredge up the will to withstand the raucous energy that barrages her during the holiday gatherings and festivities, let alone host them.

So, what can you do for her? Plenty. You can remember that it is natural for her to feel miserable. It is normal for her to need solitude and companionship all at the same time. Her weariness is as much a part of grieving as her tears. Remember, you are not causing her suffering, nor do you have any power to abolish it. You must let it be.

And be very careful not to signal or imply that she should brighten up and return to her old self. You would be unwittingly imposing the greatest burden on her. She will heal and be herself again. But only after she has done grieving. Perhaps next year, but not now.

So here is what to do. Host the gatherings elsewhere. Bring her to them—do not make her drive or travel alone. Keep the gathering small. Keep the noise level down. Include only people who will be nurturing and comforting to her. Avoid new names to remember and be polite to. Small children will charm her, but she will need a quiet place to retreat from them, too. Most importantly, give her permission to be sad this holiday season. (I guarantee you that if you do not follow these suggestions, she will prefer to not come.)

Reassure her the family will be just fine, even while grieving—that family togetherness is more important than holiday cheer—that she can weep, laugh, go for a walk, rest in the back bedroom, or help out in the kitchen, whenever she needs to. Tell her that you have no idea what she is going through, but you want to stand by her. Assure her that her suffering is appropriate and temporary, that you will keep the holidays, and she will want to join in again for the holidays to come.

And please do not be frightened or offended if she says "no." Her instincts might tell her to stay home this year, alone, where everything is familiar, quiet, and full of memories, to curl up on the sofa in his robe and weep for her lost love.

HEALING HOLIDAYS

How else can you harbor and comfort your newly widowed mom during this difficult first holiday season without Pops?

Here is how: keep Pops' memory alive and kicking. Your tendency is to protect her by NOT mentioning him. And every minute she is just waiting to hear his name, hoping for you to include him, as always, in your conversation. You could also initiate a new holiday custom in his honor, such as:

Candles—keep one big fat candle burning constantly as Pops' light. When everyone comes, each can bring a candle to light off his, and place around the room (or in a box of sand set out for that purpose).

Pictures—hot cider, popcorn, and pictures. Review the family albums, slides, movies, videos, remembering family gatherings with Pops. Or simply encourage each person to tell their favorite holiday memory, or the story behind each old family ornament. Perhaps record them as Mom's Christmas present.

Tattling—encourage everyone to tell on Pops. Take turns recounting little details each can remember about his bloopers, best moments, most annoying habits, greatest kindnesses. (Like his denial of snoring on the sofa after big family dinners or of trimming his nose hairs. Like his comb-over, or the ratty old wallet, or a pint of Guinness every evening before bed, or proudly giving the grandkids a quarter to go shopping now that nothing costs less than a buck. How about the littlest guy's fascination with watching Pops use the bathroom? Or the time his daughter caught the biggest fish and he got testy? Or the time he took his granddaughter on a practice first date?)

Prizes—give a prize for the best imitation of his snore, his shaving, his eating or driving habits. How did he grip the steering wheel? Get the teenagers to create a Pops trivia game (about his nicknames—how he got them, how he reacted to them—and nicknames he gave each family member, about his military experiences, or first jobs, list colors and makes of his vehicles, or names and breeds of his dogs, etc.).

Create a new way to keep him somehow with you during the holiday season. Make his name a household word. Make his favorite dish. Have a moment's ceremony to pass on his old turkey-carving knife to the next one in line. The centerpiece on the table could be arranged in his raunchy old fishing hat, or around his favorite golf-club. Or perhaps a simple but lovely bouquet of his most worn down wrenches and screwdrivers. His bereaved wife will be smiling through her tears. And so glad she came.

If her bereavement is too raw for any of this—the key is simplicity, and togetherness. Pancakes in the kitchen, but together. Sitting in the dark at a Christmas concert, but together. Midnight candlelight church service, instead of Santa Claus, but together. Inviting no friends over, just the immediate family playing cards, or lighting Hanukah candles and singing, together. A trip to the cemetery with a beautiful autumn bouquet of dried fall leaves, seed-pods and pomegranates, telling him how much you miss him this season, but together. And deep in her heart beneath the sorrow, mom may find solace this holiday season.

HEY! Instead of waiting until someone dies, start some new customs now. How about initiating some new family games of appreciation, recognition and remembrance?

Happy holidays!

HOLIDAY STRATEGIES

Is the holiday rush overwhelming you? If you are laboring under day and night family caregiving, having a new baby, learning a new job, moving to a new house, receiving a life-threatening diagnosis, breaking up with a partner of 25 years, or grieving the death of someone close— you might need to be excused from holiday obligations. By reducing holiday 'shoulds' you can reduce holiday stress.

Instead of sending Christmas cards, send Happy New Year notes in January – snail mail or electronically.

Reduce the need to put on a happy smiling face when you don't feel cheerful: decline invitations; attend only the holiday gatherings that really draw you.

Reduce the need for scrupulous housecleaning and masterful cooking by letting family gather at the in-laws' this year, with each assigned to a holiday dish.

Reduce decorations to just one room, or only the tree, or a smaller tree, or no outdoor lights, or just candlelight and a fragrant bough.

Leave the Christmas baking to the bakery, to some other grandma, to the church bake-sale.

Reduce Christmas shopping:

- no longer exchange gifts with adults
- shop from catalogues or the web
- in their names give to a charity
- send a check or gift certificate or magazine subscription
- open a savings account for the little guy, and on every gift occasion, deposit more towards a first car

Reduce the dilemma of the children's need for holiday cheer by spending the holidays with people who CAN be jolly for them, CAN make it an upbeat time for the kids while you just watch. As long as you are present, cheery or not, they'll be OK.

Reduce family focus on material goods by gifting each member with a rain-check for a special day alone with you next year: a day of shopping with the granddaughter; a day at Chuck E Cheese's with the little guy; a day at the museum; a day sorting family photos with the folks or cleaning their garage; a car wash/wax/tire rotation/oil change for the single mom; a baking day to teach a teen to bake a pie from scratch; a day to polish all the old man's shoes or the family silver; a boat trip to Catalina or whale-watching; zoos, galleries, sports events; the Sequoias; a day at Magic Mountain; a day of skiing, surfing, or fishing together.

Reduce holiday drinking and overeating by simpler homespun projects—advent calendars, cookie baking and decorating, making a miniature village of candy houses, setting out the nativity scene with Christmas readings; making the nativity figures; caroling, storytelling, seasonal books or videos.

Reduce the power of the advertising industry over you to 'buy, buy, buy' by reducing use of TV, and initiating more holiday customs of your own device. A present does not have to be gift-wrapped—YOU ARE THE GIFT—to be shared throughout the coming year as you begin to feel better. Most kids would rather spend a whole day with you, one-on-one, than have you away shopping. If not, perhaps a fresh look at the family values, the health of your relationships, could be your (unseen) holiday gift this year.

Of course, you can also reduce it to nothing. If you are so ill or bereft or otherwise unavailable—there's nothing wrong with giving each person a check to shop the after-Christmas sales, and letting it all go until next year. Explain simply and honestly to each one—kids are resilient.

Or reduce activities to the original spiritual meaning behind the holiday. Develop home customs around that, lighting more candles, playing more music and listening quietly, relishing scriptures, prayer, and contemplation, putting an arm around whomever is there, and just loving.

HOMEWORK-18: Consider two changes to your holiday customs—two things to simplify, ease, or deepen your next holiday season.

HOLIDAY HEROES

During the holidays, the unsung heroes are each of us, you and I!

Resisting inordinate intake of fats, sweets, booze, and chocolate, ah … is heroic effort enough. But more Herculean is living with the disappointment.

Disappointment? Yes, the big difference between the way Norman Rockwell saw the season of cheer, and the way we see it now. Grabby children, painful overspending, too much STUFF and then more added, the little war zones when the extended family gathers. All come, even the ones you abhor, lounging, munching, spilling drinks or getting drunk, and the awful RUSHING, crowding, and din of it all.

Or the chasm between the Hallmark card family living room on TV, and our own. Perhaps nearly empty, our living room is bereft of the folks overseas, of the kids out of range of affordable flight tickets or obligated to join the step-in-laws instead, or worse, we've outlived the best of them.

For those of us who are struggling with serious illness, or are recently bereaved—holiday time is a dreaded nightmare—without that cherished loved one here to hug, tease, open your handmade gizmo, eat your pecan pie.

All of us, you and I, are encouraged, for our own health of body and spirit, to reduce the busy chores, drop all 'shoulds,' and get back to the holiday basics. Call on someone who needs you. Feed a hungry neighbor in your area—no need to send abroad. Cherish your dear ones still alive. Hold them, sing carols with them, pray with them, eat a healthy, lovely, leisurely meal with them, see the sparkle of candlelight reflected in their eyes.

Consider lighting those red candles on your coffee table for yourself, sitting with them in silence. Simmer down a bit and remember what we are all about: Gratitude. Peace. Holiness. LOVE.

Spend less time shopping for presents and more time giving of your presence. Hold hands with a very, very old person. Find a moment to cherish a child. There are plenty of them. Any child will do.

Peace on earth. Good will among all people.

NEW YEAR'S PRAYER

I am grateful there is still enough food on earth to feed us all. I pray we distribute it.

I am grateful we have the means to humanely limit our species. I pray we accomplish it now.

I am grateful our planet is still so splendidly beautiful. I pray for our ability to let it remain so.

I am grateful that we are evolving into a society which labels its transgressions as 'dysfunction,' 'rape,' "abuse,' 'violence.' I pray those words become obsolete.

I am grateful for divine grace. I pray we stop thinking we are better than the other guys.

I am grateful for the freedom, the self-determination our forefathers carved out for us. I pray we manage to restore it.

I am grateful for living in the most affluent society on earth. I pray that EVERYONE UNDER THE SUN enjoy good water, shelter, food, cleanliness, and love.

I am grateful for the generous Americans who want to help others. I pray we heal our own festering ghettos, before we go after the flaws in other countries.

I am grateful for the advanced techniques of modern medicine. I pray they might become available to everyone.

I am grateful for our comfortable, peaceful, scenic, affluent way of life. I pray that it inspires us enough to drop our sense of entitlement.

I am grateful to those who are contributing to good will and well-being in their communities, and therefore on earth. I pray their successors uphold that kindness.

I am grateful for the patience and tolerance of my friends, co-workers and kinfolk.

I am grateful that in my 60's I have not yet lost all my bones and memory. I pray I do not outlive them.

Have you formulated your gratitudes and intentions for the year? Happy New Year!

Better yet, HAPPY NEW MOMENT!!!

HOMEWORK-19: Make a list of all your gratitudes, and savor them; do some thanking.

Chapter 11

HOW TO HELP?

"I Don't Know What to Say..."

How to comfort an acutely bereaved friend, someone who has lost a partner or a child?

LISTEN.

Do not tell him your sad stories; just LISTEN to his.

Do not stop his tears. Relish them, and shed some of your own, while you LISTEN to him.

Mention by name the person he lost, frequently, and something you liked about her, and then LISTEN to him.

If you try to make his pain go away with platitudes, false cheer or false faith, you are NOT LISTENING.

If you try to distract him from his sorrow, you are trying the impossible, and forcing him to hide it for you, because the message he gets is that you cannot stand to be around his grief. And that makes him very lonely. Better to just allow him to grieve and LISTEN to him.

But he is saying nothing? Do not fill the silence with your own stories—LISTEN to the silence and BREATHE deeply.

If he says he is just fine, stand by anyway (because he really is not). Do not judge his 'denial,' just LISTEN to it.

Denial immediately after a tragedy is a normal and necessary survival tool. Denial will recede naturally as he accomplishes his mourning and becomes able to tolerate the news. The bereaved might tell you with his mouth that someone died, but in his heart, he does not really get it. Do not question his stance; gently model your own acceptance of the facts; and trust the wisdom of his body to know when his natural anesthetic can wear off.

For a year, keep giving him permission to be miserable. Stand by if he complains and weeps and refuses invitations. Respect his privacy and listen to him. Call him on the phone and listen to him. Acknowledge the enormity of his loss, the appropriateness of his deep sorrow.

As he begins to show interest in his world again, sit next to him at church, or walk the beach with him, and LISTEN.

Remind him that although the change in his life is permanent, adjusting to his new world as it is now, is a process which will finish— that this grieving is temporary. Remind him that in this first year he is likely not to have the extra energy to make good decisions, that it is crucial he leave big life changes until next year. That it is time to let other things coast along; that his only real job in this first year is to mourn, to be miserable, and to survive.

And later when he finds that he IS surviving, and his energy is returning, help him find meaningful new projects—volunteering, or model railroading, or going back to school, or finding a new job or even a new partner.

Get him to help you paint your house. Friendly banter? A bit is good. And then? LISTEN.

HOMEWORK-20: Trade listening with a friend— over coffee or a glass of wine or a cold beer.

A) You tell him/her about your day, or better, the highlights and lowlights of your life so far (whatever might flash before your eyes if you fell off a cliff). Then he tells you his.

B) Or you think of three things you would abhor about your own memorial, and three things you would like. Share these with the person closest to you, and hear what his/hers are.

Then critique the experience—were you each given eye contact, really HEARD? Or judged?
Then, practice listening. With everyone. With anyone. Really listening. Gathering no opinions, no feelings, no judgments. Just listening.

LIFE REVIEW

When you fall over a cliff, they say, your whole life flashes before you. Even when our life is ending more slowly, we absolutely need to go over it in our mind. In fact, even when a portion of our life is ending, we have this compulsion to review it. Maybe we simply cannot move beyond, into our future, until we have let go of our past. We need a wrap-up, a debriefing, an assessment of its failures and successes, and daily workings. Only then are we able to face the new life, the new epic, the new world without the beloved in it, the new project or assignment or passion, the new job, the new lifestyle, the new partner, the new home, the new school, the new car, the new cookie cutter.

You might not have noticed, when you were packing to move, how much 'reminiscing' you did while you chose which item to keep and which to let go of. When the groom's best friend toasts to the couple's future, he often will make some remarks about his past with his friend. When you get rid of the old sofa, you sit on it a last moment to reminisce. Sitting in the stands, watching your kid graduate, you go over in your mind all that you did to keep him safe, alive, and happy. Or, when you gave a ring to your granddaughter, you related its family history, perhaps your story of your youth. That's all life review. It's healthy and it's helpful.

Whether we are a man or a woman, whether we say it out loud or go over it in our mind—life review happens. Life review is necessary. If someone is stuck someplace, distraught about some life change, often all they need is to be prodded into reminiscing, or life review, with a simple, related, open-ended question: "How did you two first meet?" "Weren't there any good things in the marriage?" "What sort of work were you in?" "What are you most satisfied for having done?" "Was he always this tidy?" "How was she as a baby?" "How did you two survive the Depression?" "Have you ever gone camping/played a musical instrument/ entered politics/fed a hungry man/served in the military/ hitch-hiked? What was it like?"

One of the best things you can do when someone's spouse has just died—besides simply standing by, making yourself constantly available— is to listen. To keep quiet and LISTEN. With a simple question, their life review will almost uncontrollably come tumbling out. Be a willing, interested listener, with one-pointed attention and no interrupting behavior. Listen with your whole body and being. LISTEN.

Once, I sat shoulder to shoulder with a 17-year-old girl, on the ground outside the hospital where they had her baby who had just died of crib death. She was trembling. Believe me, I had NOTHING to say. Which was a blessing for her. She kept telling me what a good mommy she had been. And I just nodded and LISTENED.

GRANDMA BAKER

Grandma Baker lay on her hospital bed in the middle of the living room, semi-comatose, certainly not talking. Her family was notified this was their last chance to visit with her. They were milling around in and out of doors. One complained for the rest of them, "I just don't know what to do."

"Well," I offered, "how about tattling on Grandma? Why don't you all look at pictures and tell stories on her, right there in the living room, so she can hear you." They got out the family movies, and shared about camping trips, birthday parties, whistling at Grandma's pretty legs in shorts at the beach. Siblings joked about this twerp brother or bratty baby sister. They forgot about death and just got into Grandma's life, story after story, with giggles, and shouts. She just lay there, too weak to join in, but not missing a thing. There they all were, jolly together at Grandma's expense. She witnessed them all bonding and, in spite of all the petty feuds, being family. Grandma died a few hours later.

There are just too many coincidences—reams of stories like this. Each one of us can tell one. Goes to show—we simply die when we are satisfied that it's OK to go. When we're ready, it's easy. Perhaps that life review readied Grandma Baker.

ERIC

Eric, a younger man, was just plain angry. He sat up in his hospital bed, alone in the house, with clenched teeth and no interest in conversation. Around his bed radiated carpet marks of fresh vacuuming. I introduced myself, offered to be company if he wanted it, but he only grunted a syllable here and there. We both stared out his picture window at the stark bluffs which had been photographed by every camera that ever passed through our picturesque town. After much silence, I left with permission to return soon.

The next week, Eric's frantic little wife was just leaving for work, her house utterly immaculate, and I left fresh footprints in the vacuumed pile carpet as I pulled a chair alongside his bed. I asked if he cared to hear about the night I slept on top of the Topas. After an hour of the swallows circling beneath us, swooping into their nesting holes in the cliffs beneath us, watching the full moon swing by overhead, the clouds reflected in the still ocean beyond the hills beyond our town, the wind and the wondering if rattlers or coyotes would disturb us on our hollowed out rock .... He smiled at me and I took leave of him, with permission to return.

The next week, Eric and I were relaxed with each other. I commented about the fresh vacuum marks all around his bed. He said, "That's all she does for me. Is clean." And I realized that the poor, frightened wife was hoping to keep death at bay with her trusty vacuum. Clearly they were not talking, and the man needed someone to talk to. I guessed he needed to review his life.

"So, what kind of work were you in?" was all I said. That opened a two-hour monologue. He had worked the pipeline for the oil company, bossed a crew of men. Admitted he was a good boss, described the cats, the big equipment they operated. He wept telling me he regretted spending too much time on the job, not enough time with his kids. Wished he had more time with them when they were little. Then he remembered how he took his two little boys out to actually drive the biggest cat ... proud that he had given that chance to his boys. Then he stopped talking, satisfied with his work, pleased with his sons. At ease with his life and his death, he was tons lighter when I left. The nurses were amazed that he died easily, way ahead of expectations, two days later. He was done, did not need another vacuuming. The man was ready to go.

DON'T MOVE A WIDOW

"He meant well," is the tolerant explanation. 'Well-meaning' often translates to me as 'ignorance' or 'selfish motives.'

Take the frequent example of 'well-meaning' folks helping a new widow dispose of the deceased spouse's belongings. They want to clean up the devastation of her life as quickly as possible—so that they can get back to theirs. They want to stop her pain so that they do not have to witness it. Her children most frequently fall into this error.

When they dispose of belongings without conferring with her, without assisting her to do it herself, AT HER PACE, they are disposing of her history, and of her healthy grief-work tools. At best, they are hindering her—at worst, hurting and crippling her.

Most bereaved need to close down their old life themselves, so that they can gradually release it and turn to their new life with energy and health and peace, and eventually with enthusiasm. The helpers CANNOT SPEED UP THAT PROCESS. She needs to sort through all those memories while she sorts through his clothes. She needs to say goodbye to him with each tool sold, or vehicle, or armchair. Weeping, even raging, might be a part of that process—all balm to her wound. And she needs to do it in the home they shared, for the deepest and speediest healing.

However, she cannot express these needs. The most common VALID advice given to a newly grieving person is to "make no major changes, no major decisions, during the first year after a deep loss." Because the greatest change HAS occurred—her husband has been yanked ruthlessly out of her life— she cannot tolerate, cannot manage successfully, anything else new for at least a year.

The worst disservice—which hits the widow like abuse—is to take her from her home, disassemble it, disperse her furniture and household fixtures, then plant her in someone else's home amid the belongings of others. This pulls the rug out from under her, disorients her, displaces her, and now she is bereft not only of her life partner, but also of her own surroundings and environment, of her familiar neighbors and daily practices, of her self image. Yes, now she has been robbed of her very own self, and who she really is. Losing their home, she loses her moorings.

Sometimes there is no choice but to move her into your back bedroom, because she is impaired and, without her spouse, has no caregiver. But could you please try to leave her home intact so that she could be involved in a slow dissolution of it? Or store all her belongings in self-storage until she can face them herself? Better yet, try, try, TRY to keep her in her own home with a hired or family companion for that first year. Not as convenient for you? NO, but it is her needs we must address here, not yours. Can't afford it? Are you sure? It is worth any sacrifice to allow her time to mourn in her own place.

If her children had any idea how crushing it is for a widow to be suddenly dispossessed of her home and furnishings within the first few weeks or months of her critical loss, they would never allow it. Remember, they have only one loss—Dad. She has lost doubly. First, Dad. Second, her every moment of daily life is a shambles, her lifestyle GONE. She no longer knows how to behave among humans as a solitary figure. If, third, she loses her home—that is the 'last straw.'

So, if you know of some 'well-meaning' persons taking over for some new widow and moving her quickly into a new granny flat or a nice retirement home—it is likely for their own convenience and out of their own ignorance. The numbed, newly bereaved person—man or woman—usually passively assents, because life is suddenly empty and nothing matters anyway. S/he does not know any better, or has no heart to protest. It is like 'taking candy from a baby,' like 'hitting a man when he is down.' PLEASE TALK THEM OUT OF IT.

Or call your local bereavement counselor and let HER at them!

> *HOMEWORK-21: Locate the closest professional who specializes in bereavement counseling.*
> *Start by asking a hospital social worker, or the local hospice, or the LCSW with a visiting nursing agency.*

SOLACE IN THE WORKPLACE

"My co-worker on the job is in crisis—what can I do for him?"

You have asked a righteous question, one that is very difficult to figure out, because there are two conflicting answers. Why? Your co-worker has two conflicting needs:

1) He needs your understanding of what he is going through, your validation and support.

2) He needs to continue making his living, justifying his salary, putting all family thoughts aside in order to tough it out at work.

If you start to sympathize for #1, his armor might come down, to reveal his anguish, or his sorrow, and then he will not be able to work, #2. What to do?

Shelter him by following his lead. Listen carefully to him, and observe him, and follow his cues. If he talks about work, stay with him on work. If he talks about his sorrow, do not try to cheer him up—stay with his sorrow. If he chatters superficially—follow suit.

If tears well up about the family issue, stay with him and listen. If he disappears into the stock closet or rest room, follow him there, and be with him silently, or stay on the floor and cover for him whenever he is temporarily 'off duty.' Keep your eyes open to ways that you might take extra chores from him, cover for him when he forgets appointments or tasks, or correct his errors without calling attention to them. Allow him to coast for a while on his past work merits, while he gets through his personal grief. Keep in mind that grief is temporary, and while we are grieving, we are rendered TEMPORARILY somewhat less competent. One day you might need the same from him, or someone else, and this will be like an investment in human kindness for you.

Mention by name the person he is upset about. It is usually a comfort to someone in grief for you to name the person he has lost or is losing, and to recall a good moment with that person—whose spoken name and remembered past value are balm to his wounds and will bring a smile through his tears.

Or perhaps he is managing well in the workplace and you are concerned that he is 'in denial' of his loss, and maybe you should bring him back to reality. Nope. Denial is a useful tool for just such occasions. If he can take a break from his troubles by getting absorbed in his job, his work might be just the rest he needs. If the 'denial' is enabling him to keep functioning, keep earning his living, then it is a necessary 'denial.' I prefer to call it a 'natural anesthetic' that his own biological system knows to provide for him. Do not judge it. Let it be.

So just follow his cues. Try to set YOUR needs aside, to genuinely provide for HIS, and be sensitive enough and observant enough, and benevolent enough (we do not always like our co-workers) to know what they might be. If you need a bit of coaching on how to help him, hopefully you are free to call your local hospice grief counselor. Probably together, you and s/he could figure it out.

TERMINAL PHONE CALL

I bumped into Susan and Ed at the library, asked how they were doing, and they said they were troubled with news that someone in the family had bad cancer, lived far away, and they wanted to reach out to him and say their goodbyes. But they were scared to, afraid of offending or alarming him.

"What do we say over the phone?" they groaned. We went outside to a garden bench, and I outlined for them their phone call. The next time I saw them in town, they glowingly thanked me for their very satisfying last conversation with the relative.

My advice was this:

Keep it short. Get his views, don't push yours. Use easy language you are both used to. Remember both you and he, until your last breath, are very much present and accounted for. He might be dying soon. But then again, so might you. Now he is alive, and he is the same person he was before he got sick. He is likely tired of people circling around him, talking behind his back, keeping secrets, deciding for him. Remember that he is alive and you EMPOWER HIM by seeking HIS OPINIONS.

Get his permission to talk on the phone, to ask him about his condition, to visit later, to get the info only he has, etc. Defer to his seniority, inside knowledge, opinions, mastery, etc, by 'needing' him to enlighten, teach, inform you.

So first establish with him if it's a 'good time to talk.' Establish each of your whereabouts while speaking on the phone—the visuals are good openers. Keep small talk very brief.

Quickly get to your reason for calling—that you've heard bad news, and you need to get HIS scoop directly—both what the physician tells him, AND more importantly, how he himself sees his future.

Mention his contributions to your life. Anything you can appreciate. Take a breath and give him a chance to continue with some life review, or not.

Say goodbye, in case it's your last chance. (I always finish with "see you later," because here and hereafter are pretty much the same to me.)

So here's a sample phone call:

Hello, Uncle Henry, Susie here. Got a minute to talk?

Sure, what's up?

I'm having my second cup of coffee at my kitchen table, looking out on a nice sunny day. I'm wondering, where are you?

On the sofa.

Can you see the trees out the window? Is it snowing?

Yup, been snowing for two days, no trees to see—especially when I'm dozing.

How's that, are you sick?

Just tired.

Around here they're talking about you. I don't believe second-hand information, so I need to ask you directly what's going on. May I?

Ask away.

Why are they saying "terminal illness," Uncle Henry?

Cuz I got the cancer.

Ooooh, that's serious. What does the doc say about that?

Says I got it all over. Nothing he can do.

Well, but that's the doc's opinion. You've got the inside scoop. How do YOU see it?

I won't be here for Christmas.

Ooooh. Nooooo. (Silence … take a breath) Are you ready for that?

Got my will. I want a military funeral. Kids already have the house.

Sounds like you're all packed, ready to go. (silence)

Well, you've accomplished a lot in your years.... (silence)

I'll miss fishing with you. Some of the best times of my life have been camping at the lake with you.... (Silence … take a breath)

Could I come visit and get one of your (smooches), (beers), (hugs), (watch a ballgame on the tube like we used to) while the gettin's good?

Don't go out of your way. I'm not much company these days.

Are you hurting?

Got medicine for pain, so I sleep a lot.

Any chance I could bring those old family photos and have you tell me who those folks are, between naps, so I can label them on the back? It would be a huge help.

This medicine makes me groggy.

Maybe you won't feel up to it. That's OK. We'll see when I get there. I'll be out your way for a book conference anyway. May I stop by?

Sure, you come when you can.

Thanks for talking, Uncle Henry. I feel much better now—I hate being in the dark.

You're welcome, kiddo.

See you later.

Another sample phone call:

Hi, Hanna, may I speak to Sam?

No, the nurse is with him right now.

I'll call back. What time of day is best for him?

Evening.

OK, you get back to him. Bye.

(Next evening)

Hey, Sam, you old stinker, how's your poker game?

Not playing much ... lately.

How come?

Not up to par.

Not feeling well?

Nope. The doc says I'm terminal.

What's that mean? Sounds like a bus station.

I'm gonna die.

We're all gonna die, Sam, even that doc of yours.... But do you mean you're gonna die soon?

Yup.

Oooh....(Silence) How's that working out for you, Sam?

OK. Nurse got me to talk to a free lawyer. Wife's gonna sell my truck and get herself a little sedan.

How's she doing?

Not good.

Listen, we can stand by her. Do you want us to come out now and visit?

Nope. Sounds too much like work, visitors.... She'll need you worse when I'm gone. Come then.

When do think that'll be?

Doc said less than six months—a few weeks ago.

Yeah, but what does he know? You're in there, Sam, I'd trust your take on it more than the doctor's. What's your guesstimate?

(Silence. . .) Well, I won't be here for Christmas.

(Silence...) I'm going to miss you.... Remember how mad I got when you plowed down my mailbox when the cement wasn't even set yet?

How can I forget?

I was mad at you for nearly a year.

Yup, I knew. You wouldn't look me in the eye.

Well, if I never said it, I forgive you, Sam.

That's a relief. I'd hate a lawsuit now.

Etc....

NO FUNERAL FOR ME!

"No funeral for me! No service of any kind!"

This remark raises the hackles of a bereavement counselor, because it causes her so much more work. Because the absence of a funeral leaves everything nebulous, leaving the bereaved unmoored, adrift and lost. People who, like my own parents did, forbid a gathering of any kind, really cannot predict what we folks left behind might need.

They have many 'good reasons':

"It's morbid." But that is the nature of death. Death means morbid. So admit it. Acknowledge the death of the physical body and dispose of it. Celebrate the life of the spirit, or the lifespan of that unique personality, so you can move on.

"It's no fun. People should be happy, not sad." So have exquisite music, uplifting poetry. Or an 'Irish Wake' with food and ale. But have something, some marker of the event.

"No speeches about me by somebody hired to talk who never knew me." So make and keep some friends who will cherish you and survive you to speak knowingly and glowingly of you later. Or write down your own self-truths to be read. One woman I knew recorded her own remarks and life review, to be played at the end of her service. SHE had the last word!

"No meeting in the dead-body warehouse." So indicate a tree out under the sky, or somebody's boat. Or your own house where they knew you well. There's nothing wrong with church, either.

"No awful organ music." So think of a guitar. Travels everywhere. Or bagpipes and drum. A sweet flute. Rock 'n 'roll records? How about everybody just singing their hearts out with some rousing songs?

"I don't want anyone talking about me." YOU do not have to be listening. Your bereaved friends will need to hear each others' experiences of you. Your bereaved partner gets to know you from a greater perspective than just his/her relationship with you. Which serves as a powerful LIFE-REVIEW to enable letting go of you. Done well, the sharing can provide enormous relief for the bereaved. It is not for you.

"I don't want any tears." Our society is irrationally abhorrent of tears. Beats me why. Your memorial is, in fact, the only place where tears ARE socially allowed. Crying is exhausting, but we were invented with tear ducts for good reason. Among sympathetic folks, mutual crying draws the additional energy of kinship and encouragement from hugs, handshakes, deep looks. And crying is a tremendous release.

"I don't want people to be sad." But the purpose of a gathering in the name of the deceased is to launch the mourning process—which is the project of adjusting to the landscape of life without you in it. If people liked you, they will miss you for a while, which might make them sad. This gathering, or the public disposition of the remains, is the jump-start, the ignition of healthy grieving, of the letting go and getting on with life. Without that permission, grief can get stuck in the craw. Mourning amongst others who also knew the deceased is a way of giving the bereaved communal verification that in fact death occurred, and giving tacit societal permission to live on without that person. A funeral is the community dissolution of all the contracts people had with you, just as a wedding is also a public dissolution of previous social contracts. (Remember the saying of the banns as part of the marriage contract, and "Speak now or forever hold your peace"?)

Perhaps the memorial at death is the most health-giving of all our life-transition rituals. Those who do not attend the gathering suffer more or longer than those who attended. Festering grief might transmit as panic attacks, depression, bitterness, impatience with others who do grieve, hostility, drug-seeking, acting out, perhaps even violence. Many (if not all) body ailments might be an extension of 'stuffed' grief which could have been released all at once by lamenting and sobbing it out at the socially acceptable event for that, the funeral.

A funeral, like surgery, isn't pretty at the time, but sure can improve our health.

So, when you die, your funeral might not do YOU much good, but it provides, for those who knew you, much needed emotional and physical support. It gives them closure—a chance to experience and express the pain of their loss, their joy at still being alive, and merriment over their times with you. Allow them the chance to be sad and glad together.

I have found that those who do not attend a public mourning ritual for you, might need to devise a good-bye ritual of their own in order to get through their grief. So, at the time that you forbid a funeral of any sort, kindly recommend good bereavement counseling to your survivors. They are going to need it.

> *HOMEWORK-22: Plan your own MEMORIAL (wake/goodbye party/celebration/funeral). Some people plan in detail; others just say, "Throw a party for me," or "Do as you wish. I don't care, since it's for you, not for me." (Most families are VERY relieved to find some guidelines.) Whatever they are, record your own preferences, date your ideas, file them in Vital Info, but give your loved ones permission to follow them as they wish, or not.*

SUPPORT GROUPS

Mary's family berated her for keeping his clothes—but she could not get rid of them yet. Only two months since Ed had died, her heart was already broken enough. Immersed in sorrow and bewilderment, she managed to find her way to a grief support group. There she heard that one widow got rid of her husband's clothes the day after he died, while another bereaved wife still had ALL his things intact a full year after her husband had died. Mary learned that getting rid of a beloved's belongings IS monumental, and cannot be done until she herself is ready to do so.

John thought it was a death sentence. After he complained of unexplainable fatigue, his doctor called him with test results diagnosing Hepatitis C. Panicked, he attended a meeting of a support group for people with his illness. He met many other people who were under treatment, finished with treatment, deciding about treatment. They were all very much alive, and his relief was visible. John returns each month—slowly learning about symptoms, treatment options, attitudes and strategies that others have used since their diagnosis. And his fear is under control.

Mildred, a devoted wife, is killing herself with sleep deprivation, heavy lifting, daily hard work around the clock, and the loneliness of living with someone with dementia. Emotionally in despair, she is watching the living death of the man she married fifty years ago, who no longer knows her name or how to get dressed or use a toilet. In the Caregivers Support Group she is learning to take care of TWO people, herself being one of them. She is learning to accept help, and to develop her own interests away from her patient. Mildred is redefining loyalty to her husband—it means taking good care of his wife so that he can have her good care until he dies.

At volunteer hospices, there might be support groups for people grieving the loss of a husband, the loss of a wife, the loss of a child, loss due to suicide or to violence, the sorrow of caring for a loved one with Alzheimer's or Parkinson's, the loss of one's own lifestyle or marriage or career to fibromyalgia, the loss of self-image and trust due to breast cancer, the loss of one's freedom while care-giving a dependent elder. Each troubled person who enters laden with sadness and helplessness leaves the meeting buoyant and encouraged, often laughing. People attending support groups return to their lives able to breathe more deeply and manage better. HOW IS THAT FOR SUPPORT?!

If you have a dilemma, and wonder how others manage a similar situation, or even feel you are the only one who cannot seem to get it right ... ask for a support group to be gathered around your particular issue, at your local volunteer hospice.

BEREAVED PARENTS

If you or I were to have a child, give birth to that child, feed it and protect it, and one innocent day, someone spoke the unspeakable, saying that that child had just died—what would we do? I imagine doing nothing except curling up under covers and shivering, my mind gone numb, my life gray and empty. How could I function when my heart had just been ripped out of my chest?

We humans are resilient. Amazingly, and to our dismay, most of us do not die of grief. And even more surprising, in the midst of this terrible agony—this biological horror of outliving our own child—people might actually comfort us. Which people? Only—and I repeat ONLY—other parents whose child had died would be trusted. I would need other bereaved parents—along with my own inner resolve, my native courage, my natural will to live, and my foolish willingness to go on loving.

Years ago, some parents whose child had died came to me, and together we started a monthly support group for others like them. Granted, some people came and left disappointed because their needs were not met by the group. But most parents returned month after month, year after year, at first to receive solace, then to continue providing that comfort for others. People came for an hour or two, whether it was 3 or 13 people, parents and step-parents, and later bereaved siblings as well— to bring their pain, to be heard, to learn about the biological responses to grief in a human being, to better cope, to be relieved of some of the burden of their loss, to be encouraged to manage tomorrow. Slowly, together, their wounds were healing. They were finding energy again for their other loved ones who were still alive. After a few years, the support group dissolved and people moved on.

Then, when some newly grieving parents called in, some people from the earlier groups returned to embrace them. There is no comfort greater than sitting and quietly talking with another who is suffering the same loss, and especially with another whose energy and peace have finally returned.

In these support groups, as the bereaved families looked back to events just before that child's untimely death, they would notice an uncanny leave-taking, or last triumph, as I call it—a kind of graduation, which meant that perhaps the young person had accomplished what s/he came for and died somehow complete, no matter what the age. Bereaved people contemplate these stories they share and find solace.

One bereaved mother told us that her 17-year-old son, a week or two before his fatal car accident, sat at her kitchen table and described to her in detail, out of the blue, the 'Viking funeral' that he would like to have someday. A teenager admitting death!! Doesn't happen very often. And as if he would go before his own mother's death?

SIMON CRANE

Just days before he accidentally drowned at ten years old, Simon Crane greeted nearly everyone he knew in town on a long slow walk to the ice cream store for a cone. Then, the Sunday before his death he stood up in church and gave an impromptu short talk on the Resurrection. A ten-year-old-boy knew? And made sure to comfort his kindred before leaving. His parents, Peter and Mary Crane, wrote this letter to all bereaved parents:

"We lost our son eleven years ago and joined the support group shortly thereafter. We weren't particularly optimistic that a group could help, because after all, we had suffered a loss so utterly devastating that we were 'doomed' to live out the rest of our lives in pain and sorrow. Thankfully we were wrong. We came together with other parents with whom we could share our anguish and who would show us that life can still be enjoyed, that the world is still a beautiful place and that we can carry on. Ultimately it does not matter how a child dies, but how we learn to live with it. Our group does not judge, but is here to empathize—solely to give love and support."

Please find a support group in your area for anyone you might know who is mourning the death of a child. Or start one, preferably with a professional facilitator. The comfort people gleaned from the Cranes and other parents, was immeasurable.

GRIEF OF KIDS

"Children don't grieve."

"Children should be kept away from the deathbed of their loved one, and from the funeral."

"Adults should never grieve in front of children."

"Only their parents can protect children from the pain of sorrow."

These harmful misconceptions probably reinvent themselves out of our own vulnerability and fear—unsubstantiated fear. Fear that our children will be permanently damaged by loss, by the grief around them. Fear that grief lasts forever. Fear of letting our children down. Fear that we will be asked questions we cannot answer. Fear that in acknowledging the child's grief, our unresolved grief from our own childhood will surface and overcome us. Fear that we adults are supposed to have all the answers about life and death. Fear that our child's simple candor about the loss will offend someone. Fear of rejection when the kids just want to go out and play or when they refuse to talk about the loss upon command.

There is no protection from loss. Loss occurs throughout life. Grief is simply the adjustment from the way our world used to be, to survival in our new world. Adapting ourselves to a world without that someone or something in it, is healthy. WE ALL GRIEVE. Even brand-new humans grieve.

WE MIGHT OVERLOOK THE CHILD'S GRIEF BECAUSE:

1. Kids copy us. We hide our grief from the children. This implies that grieving is wrong, and deprives children of models of healthy grief.

2. Kids grieve differently from adults—in shorter increments, through play, creative expression, ritual, mimicry, nightmares, as well as talk and tears. A kid might address the topic with a sentence or two, then skip out to play dolls or shoot hoops,

leaving us launching into a discussion with which the kid has already finished.

3. If it is a family bereavement, others are grieving too, and the young of the human species tend to put their grief on hold—go into a freeze position until they feel safe, that is, until we older family members have accomplished our grieving.

4. 'Busy work' when we are first bereaved (the logistics of gathering relatives for burial; of finding income when daddy leaves; of moving out during marital crisis) helps us to tolerate the intensity of the initial sorrow. Sitting quietly with the child's needs only drives us back into that terrible ache, so we avoid it unwittingly, and stay busy, sending the kids out to play when they are needing to be held.

5. As a primal survival tactic, human young tend to take responsibility for the job of diversion—distracting the other family members from pain. So while the child is bickering or whining about inessentials, acting out, bedwetting, getting into fights, flaunting drugs or sex—it might be an instinctive protective family survival tool.

6. If we cannot tolerate the child's fresh candor on the topic, we squash the interaction. The child therefore feels isolated and disenfranchised, and withdraws further. So we figure that young person 'doesn't care,' 'doesn't understand,' or 'isn't grieving,' and we turn to the 'more important' issues at hand.

Is YOUR child grieving? ANY child you care about?

A) Has a friend (or pet) unexpectedly died or moved away, and the child is expressing grief with tears, withdrawal, clinging, lack of appetite or energy?

B) Is a parent or sibling or mentor dying from a terminal illness, and the child having trouble with schoolwork and attendance?

C) Has a student died by suicide, and peers are confused and angry?

D) Was a student disabled or killed by student violence, and now school evokes fear?

E) Is the child's family in crisis? Marital abuse, divorce proceedings, family homelessness, parental imprisonment—or any other such loss of safety?

WHAT DO OUR GRIEVING OFFSPRING NEED MOST?

1. They need for us to not lie to them. (No euphemisms, no religious platitudes, just the facts.) Tell the truth, as far as they want to know. If the truth is "I don't know," say that.
2. They need honest answers to their questions, clear explanations of what to expect at the deathbed, in the funeral home, at the service, in court, or in the daily routine without that person around any more.
3. They need their loss acknowledged.
4. They need us to learn about their experience of grief.
5. They need us to pay attention, take the time, and LISTEN.
6. They need to mourn at their own pace until they resolve the grief by learning new ways to manage without that person. Their newly found self-confidence—the by-product of good grief—will recharge their healthy enthusiasm for life.

Overwhelmed? Good news: an outside source of support CAN really help our children. School staff, the spiritual community, or a hospice bereavement program CAN rally for the child. Meeting, playing, and talking with peers often provide, without your awareness, the needed solace and comfort for the child or teen. Nevertheless, I invite you to engage community support for your child or adolescent.

Find a student grief group, so that students suffering a loss can come together with a therapist who specializes in grief of children and teenagers. Kids can find normalcy and comfort among their grieving peers, in a safe place where their grief is recognized and resolved. Insist on it in your schools; it can happen there, as it does in ours. Most schools are willing to have programs for 'at risk' children: kids who are on the verge of drugs or dropping out, or whose families have known bad problems. If kids are not safe in their neighborhoods or homes, their lack of trust is a terrible loss. Although some troubled kids might need psychiatric treatment, MOST 'at risk' young people are suffering loss and are in need of a voice. They need validation and better outlets for their grief. Call your nearest volunteer hospice, and then call them again. Some schools are just getting started; you can help launch this kind of support in your community!

A FRIEND INDEED

How can I be a good friend for someone with a chronic illness!? Either I feel like my sick friends are avoiding me, or I become impatient and avoid them! And THEY often complain that their illness ruins relationships, including marriage and FRIENDSHIPS. So, I asked a dear friend, "HOW can I be your friend when you always seem to be under the weather and unavailable?" Linda wrote, for all of us, a list of ways. Here it is—for you who have friends who live with fibromyalgia/chronic fatigue syndrome, or perhaps any lifestyle-altering, for-the-rest-of-your-life, debilitating disease, such as Parkinson's, multiple sclerosis, rheumatoid arthritis, ALS, emphysema, COPD, or even those undergoing cancer treatments, too.

Linda's suggestions for her friends:

1. Let me know BY PHONE MESSAGE if you are thinking of me, or wanting to include me in something, or just to say "Hi."

2. Just because I LOOK good, doesn't mean I FEEL good. Pain, or weakness, or fatigue don't always show. Neither does the financial depletion caused by inability to work a job.

3. Don't assume I CAN but am refusing out of some perversity (because I look good, or because I was able yesterday). Don't assume I CAN'T, then omit inviting me (because I just refused something else). Let ME be the judge of my condition moment by moment—to figure out what I can do. No, I can't help you move, but I can hold your floor plan and tell movers where things go. I can't go cycling or surfing or hiking, but maybe I can eat with you afterwards. Please don't leave me out of your plans.

4. Ask how I am, when you care to, and educate yourself on the symptoms of my illness, so that I can use short phrases to describe how I am feeling at that moment. In return, I will try to give an accurate, simple reading of my present condition, (keeping separate my physical issues from my state of mind, such as "too tired to get out of bed, but I'm inspired by a wonderful book." Or "terribly discouraged, but I think I could manage a walk.")

5. Invite me to SHORT events, such as a lecture or concert, a walk

on the beach or in the rain, a sunset on the hilltop. Spur-of-the-moment invitations are great if you can understand that 50 percent of the time I may not answer the phone, because 50 percent of events scheduled in advance, I will need to cancel. Notice! 50 percent I CAN do. You need tolerance.

6. Let me know where your boundaries lie regarding taking me to the E.R. at our local hospital, or helping me up if I fall at home. I have a few people to choose from already.

7. Tell me good book and video titles. Discuss them or watch them with me occasionally.

8. Confide in me YOUR personal life & trials—friendship goes both ways.

9. Share your spiritual/psychological growth experiences.

10. Remember the frustration and discouragement that I must manage along with my disease, so don't take it personally if I seem unpleasant or withdrawn.

11. Don't try to fix me, and then get discouraged and leave me. Remain my patient, loyal friend, standing by for my good days. THANK YOU.

HOW CAN I HELP?

"What do I say to my grieving friend?"

"How can I help my dying friend?"

These are the two most frequent questions heard in a hospice counseling office. Surprisingly, the two answers are the same!

Whether your friend herself is dying, or her husband has just died, her life as she has known it is over. Either way, she is in a twilight zone, and needing much help. It is amazing how little help people get when they are in this acute crisis—mostly because others do not know what to do. So, here's what:

1. Ask HER. Use the phone. Or drop by and ask through the screen door. Remember, she is still alive.

2. Keep phone calls and visits very short. Do not burden her with your stories/problems/health history/complaints.

3. If you say, "Call me if there's anything you need," mean it.

Answer your phone, do what is asked, immediately.

4. If you cannot mean it—then make SPECIFIC offers instead, such as:

   - I can walk the dog tomorrow.
   - Here is some food (for the helpers surrounding her, if not for her—in throwaway containers, please)
   - Shall I pick up your son/sister at the bus/airport?
   - Shall I sit with the patient, or accompany the bereaved while funeral plans, or legal arrangements, are made?
   - I'm going to the market; what can I pick up for you?
   - Shall I take a load of stuff to the trash/thrift shop/laundry?
   - My gardener/handyman/mechanic/housekeeper is coming tomorrow—may I send him to your house instead?
   - I'm not a caregiver, but I can sit in the front room to receive visitors or deliveries, answer the phone, sort belongings, prepare a meal, scrub the bathroom, etc.

5. Do not pressure her to eat, to accept a visit, etc. Let her pace her social life and withdraw as she needs.

6. When she has energy, help her finish projects, correspondence, designate where belongings go (at her pace), or contact distant people for good-byes. It will all overwhelm her, but you can follow through on her lead.

7. Send her a letter or reminisce in person about your times with her, or with the deceased, appreciating their contributions.

8. The most needed: take shifts as caregiver during the dying, or sleep over for a few days with the newly bereaved.

9. Always be available to stimulate and LISTEN to 'life review.'

10. The most difficult: When the time is right, let go of your dying friend. Assure her that you will carry on. Give permission to let go. Stand by your grieving friend, even when her grief seems intolerable to you. Notice your needs (to have her as she used to be), then set them aside. Look her in the eye, open your heart to her suffering and just keep standing by.

11. Slow down, sit quietly, pay attention, and LISTEN, LISTEN, LISTEN.

12. Do not chatter. Listen to your heart and hear your friend. LISTEN. And if you simply cannot, if you are just too upset, call another friend to support YOU, to listen to you.

13. Call hospice. They can comfort you, encourage you, coach you and guide you.

14. You will manage just fine.

HOMEWORK-23: Interview a (not freshly) widowed friend about what were the most helpful things that people did for them during their grief. Then, find a recently widowed acquaintance and practice one of these tips. If you know of someone who is dying, can you practice one of these tips with them?

Chapter 12

CALL HOSPICE
"But I'm Not Dying"

"Anyway, we don't have hospice in our town, do we?"

"Yes, you might. Look up 'hospice' in the phone book, or call the social worker or chaplain or discharge planner in your nearest hospital, or ask at church. Volunteer hospices seem to be one of the oldest and best-kept secrets in this country. But they are well worth ferreting out. They are available any time, day or night, whether you have a medical hospice or not."

"And what are these 'volunteers' paid?"

"Not a red cent. Your community supports them. Your donation is always welcome, NEVER required. They are volunteers. That's why it's called a volunteer hospice. And you also get the help of trained professional counselors at no cost to you. Volunteer hospices provide practical help, emotional comfort, and respite care for patients with a limited life expectancy. And most hospice volunteers also serve anyone who is homebound—whether ill, or impaired, or merely frail and elderly. They also provide respite care—sitting with the homebound so the care-giving relative can take a break. Trained volunteers, supervised by a professional counselor, provide these services free of charge. There is a great satisfaction in being available to your neighbors in this crucial and satisfying way."

"Do you have nurses?"

"NO. Nurses come with the medical hospice, and only when someone is dying. Your doctor has to order them, and they are reimbursed 100 percent by Medicare and offer the full range of all hospice services…"

"What is this full range of hospice services...?"

"They ... well, that's the first job of our volunteer hospice counselor—to visit with you and assuage that first anguish you feel if you have been given a life-threatening diagnosis; to help you sort out what you can do about it; help you to prioritize, and then to acquaint you with the services of a medical hospice, as soon as you should need one. We'll help you understand what they do, and how they work with us. We'll let you know when you might be eligible, how you can access them, and what else is available to you. You may have medical hospice only when you become eligible, and your doctor orders it.

"Yet, you can have a volunteer hospice services any time you choose."

HOSPICE

Hospice. Who would 'choose' it?!

It is so confusing! Just when the doc is giving us bad news anyway, our minds in a dither, who could even figure out how to get hospice? Excuse me for using that 'h' word. Even the doc gets vague about it!

How easy it would be if s/he gently said, "Look, these treatments might work, and yet this illness might eventually take your life. Why don't you go home, get some rest, and enjoy your friends and family. If it turns out that the treatments are doing you no good, we'll discontinue them and I'll send a hospice nurse so that I can be sure we are keeping you comfortable and pain-free."

Instead, it is often just up to you. So call your local volunteer hospice (no nurse, no medicine). Tell them you are at a loss and need help to figure things out. The hospice counselor will visit, hear you out, assess what might be helpful, and coach you through the steps of getting what you need. She will also assign you a volunteer who might run errands for you, or sit with the patient while you run them, or do simple tasks you can't seem to manage now, and simply be a peaceful, unalarmed presence around when you need it most.

Volunteers do this for everybody who is homebound, whether they are ill, frail elderly, just home from the hospital, temporarily injured, whatever. That calm reassurance enables you to clear your head and follow through on what needs to be done—like calling the family to rally help, or stocking up the freezer with prepared meals, or setting up a schedule for daily visits or treatments, or contacting the lawyer, accountant, or maybe the local funeral home.

Your doctor will order the hospice nurse for you—the medical hospice services—when you ask, when you become eligible by having a declining condition, when you're receiving no further curative treatments, or if he gives you that scary 'six months prognosis.' That is NOT a six-months death sentence. It is a life sentence—to live in your home, in hope and comfort (hope that nobody else dies before you do). And to laugh. Why not? Some of my deepest belly laughs have been with dying patients.

"Hospice does not add days to your life, hospice adds life to your days," said one hospice worker.

Hospice is like a wheelchair or an ambulance. We are afraid of them, but when we absolutely are forced to use them, they sure come in handy. I am suggesting you use them once in a while before you are forced to. Take turns in the wheelchair at the huge museum just to rest your feet. Or form a proud wheelchair contingent in your local 4th of July parade and travel the parade route in a wheelchair. Call hospice to attend a workshop on end of life documents, just for housekeeping, or ask them to guide you in comforting your newly bereaved friend. Better yet, volunteer for, or donate goods to your local volunteer hospice, or start one in your town if no one else has. Quickly you will lose that awful dread, and you'll travel lighter through life.

MAC

"I have to leave him. I don't know what else to do but take the kids and go to my mom's in Colorado. So, I came to you."

This young mother, shiny-haired, her legs entwined, was shredding her Kleenex. I watched the white bits fall into the grass as we sat on the lawn behind my office. Counseling people in crisis was smoother out under the sky. The tall trees dancing in the wind did half the job of soothing.

Julie's crisis was her husband's scary rage. He no longer paid any attention to their little tow-headed boys. He worked the pipeline—hard physical work—guzzled too much beer after work, and played softball with his co-workers afterwards. Then he came home to yell at his little family, occasionally threatening violence by throwing food, dashing plates against the kitchen wall.

"Get him to a doctor. Mac has radically changed, not you," was my response. I urged a full medical work-up—however she could coax him into it. His headaches convinced him. The results were devastating. A nasty brain tumor was causing his tantrums.

Mac never lost his sly wit. After months of lugging his accumulating medical files from diagnostic center to treatment center to physician to hospital (because they could not keep things straight), he was becoming the only authority on his case. The husky redheaded guy nearly died from a heart attack, caused by radical melanoma treatments. He was finally on his back in a nearby hospital, when I visited him there.

"So? Have they done the brain scan?" I asked cheerfully.

"Yup," he grumbled.

"Did they find anything?"

"Yup. They found the brain. In my head! One of the first places they looked."

How I laughed with Mac.

Until finally they resorted to brain surgery on him.

Julie begged me to help her tell Mac. So the three of us clustered in plastic chairs in the middle of my wild and beautiful lawn, where deer sometimes grazed. Mac's wife sat watching him silently, her hands still, her blue eyes dry, her tears already spent. Mac licked his beaver teeth with a tongue dried from medications.

"So?" Mac fidgeted, looking back and forth from me to Julie. "So who called this meeting of the board?"

"I did," I answered, to take the pressure off her.

"It's OK, Susie, I'll start. Honey, while you were too drugged to understand, the surgeon told us together. The tumor has taken over. Your ravaged body can't tolerate any more treatment." She took a deep breath and finished,

"Mac, you are going to die. Soon."

Silently, Mac looked to me. His eyes glittering green as prize marbles in the lowering sun, he stared into mine.

"I didn't plan on this," he murmured, without breaking his gaze. My heart pouring back into his eyes, I slowly shook my head and echoed,

"You didn't plan on this."

There were no more words.

Without a blink, his bulging eyes emitted a pair of tears.

His friends threw a city-wide fundraiser for Mac's horrendous expenses. Steaks and beer in the park. It was really a live wake. Speeches and hugs. Mac stood up to the mike to talk, but cried instead, and they lowered him from the riser in a huddle of bear-hugs.

Later, his best friend called to say, "I'm sorry, Mac; I couldn't come to see you. I can't stand this."

"Hey, man," Mac reassured him, "I don't blame you. I'd feel the same way. Don't worry about it. I just want to stay home with my kids anyway." He forgave his buddy, but he wept his loneliness as he recounted this to me.

Mac ultimately discovered that loving his children was all he wanted to do. The last time I saw him, I just stood a moment in his doorway, and he didn't speak to me. Reduced to kitten-weakness and peach-fuzz thatch, he lay in his big bed covered by rumpled sheets, with two yellow heads tumbling and burrowing like puppies. Smiling serenely, Mac just waved at me.

And that was that. He died some days later. It was a privilege to know that gallant family, to have been allowed to do the best hospice counseling of my career—which had no influence on death, but had the power to improve and sweeten the end of a good life.

DEFINE 'VOLUNTEER HOSPICE':

VOLUNTEER HOSPICE began in the late '70s as a free community service for families when someone was dying at home. Now it provides counseling and practical services for the elderly, those who are impaired or chronically ill, caregivers, and the bereaved, as well as for the sick and the dying.

(Medical Hospice began in the late '80s, providing full medical care for the dying, paid by health insurance, ordered by the physician when the patient has less than 6 months to live.)

VOLUNTEER HOSPICE still gives moral support from the time of the first serious diagnosis (long before a patient is eligible for medical hospice); still introduces the concept of hospice care to the family; still comforts, assists, and counsels during the illness—deferring to the hospice nurse in charge; still stands by the patient until s/he gets well, or vigils with the family during the dying; still stays (after the medical hospice nurse leaves) until family or neighbors arrive to stay with the freshly bereaved.

VOLUNTEER HOSPICE provides ongoing bereavement counseling and comfort for all the grief-stricken in the community, whether by sudden or expected loss—that is, whether the bereaved were using hospice care before the death, or it was a sudden accidental or violent death.

VOLUNTEER HOSPICE works adjunctively with local medical hospices, providing the required volunteer component of their care, and often much of their counseling and most of their bereavement care.

VOLUNTEER HOSPICE also might provide home assessment of any other homebound person—whether frail or impaired elderly, chronically ill or disabled—giving counsel to them and to those responsible for them.

VOLUNTEER HOSPICE sends friendly visitor volunteers to all homebound people, volunteers who can run errands for them, or sit by their side.

VOLUNTEER HOSPICE educates the community on end-of-life issues, documents, choices, and preparations. Inquire whether you could attend the volunteer training, even if you were not intending to actually volunteer. Volunteer training can be a great community education service for anyone willing to better manage, for themselves, the personal issues addressed in this book. Some of the training assignments might be some of the homework suggestions offered in this book.

HOMEWORK-24: Locate hospices in your area, get acquainted, add to your Vital Info file.

Chapter 13

PROOF

Jazzbo's Last Fling

The wind pressed her hair back as if she wore a stocking over it. Her hands clutched the iron anvil-looking bow cleat of the boat. Alone at the prow of a whale-watching boat, her face jutted into the wind, like an old galleon's maidenhead.

Jazzbo was skimming over the ocean amid a sea of dolphins, hundreds of them; a nursery pod of babies surfacing alongside mommies. She was enthralled; she couldn't wait to tell the women at her dinner table about dolphins roiling the water as far as she could see.

Once a California beach beauty who body surfed, hunted grunion by moonlight, danced on the sand, camped on beaches with her husband, Jazzbo had been taking pleasure in her Pacific Ocean for 90 years.

She had outlived him now eight years. She wondered how much longer? How could her ashes join Shoey's out there in the deep, as healthy as she still was? Without swallowing a collection of her pills, how could she die nicely, before outliving herself?

"Wait a minute," Janet ordered me. She shook the beanbag cushion under her lap board, replaced it on her lap and checked for level, then shook it again and finally wiggled it into snug position. I opened the backgammon board onto it. I drew up the low wooden chair I had sat in as a child. My knees hugged hers. We grabbed our pieces, mine ebony, hers ivory, and set up our game.

"Where'd the flowers come from, Mom?" Fragrant red garden roses dropped petals on her marble-top table.

"Management girl brought them to me." She rattled her dice like a maraca in their leather cup.

"Why?"

"Just 'cause. She knows I'll cherish them 'til the last petal falls." She smiled that casual near shrug of someone who has always been admired and approached with gifts, of that entitlement of a beautiful woman. She threw her dice.

"Doubles!"

"Now don't start that," I growled. She beamed.

My ancient mother was happy now. After the last bitter decade of family alcoholism, lashing sorrow, bone pain, surgery with nasty chronic sickness, and sudden widowhood, Janet had sold her last home, moved to Ventura to this tiny studio with an ocean view, in a residence that felt like a four-star hotel. Downstairs, in the grand circular glass dining room surrounded by lawns and trees, she ordered delicious suppers off a menu, delighted her tablemates, and quickly became, again, the prettiest, most popular of her peers, just as she had done in high school when she boggled the innocent engineering student Shoemaker with her enchanting sass and devastating beauty. Here with the excitement of creating one more charming little home, Jazzbo had blossomed into her last glorious fling of enthusiasm.

I tossed the dice barehanded onto the felt board, then reached for the shelled pistachios on her oval coffee table, glancing around at her family treasures—the Victorian love seat and chair, the grandfather clock, matching oak dressers—all refinished and reupholstered by her.

"Where's the green chair, Jazzbo?" I asked through a mouthful, as I tapped my little black disks into new positions.

"Oh, I gave that to the cleaning girl; didn't need it."

"Still paring down. Good for you! I brag about you at the senior center—how you bravely sold your last car, the red hot rod." She had progressed, since middle age, from big homes to smaller homes—cleaning out garages and closets as the stuff became obsolete.

"Takes courage to age well," I preached. The crystal she had bequeathed to her niece, Julie, the china to a sister; she had given her stainless steel to me, and kept her wedding sterling for breakfast here in her mini-kitchen.

"It's your turn, Janet.... How's your back?"

"I just took a pain pill." She lived around her back pain and her bowel issues; bounced in and out of the E.R. with dehydration or blood pressure scares. She enjoyed the doctors who oversaw her various body parts; sometimes even obeyed them. She kept her body balanced and comfortable enough—IF she remembered to drink water.

"Woo," I complained. She kept her thermostat in the 80s. "Are you warm enough?" She shot me a dirty look and clacked her dice cup. One die landed on its edge; she gathered it up and tossed it back down. I peeled off a sweatshirt.

"Why haven't you finished that sewing?" As a designer, seamstress, tailor, as well as house redecorator, she had always played a sewing machine like a concert piano; now all that was reduced to a big basket of handwork on the floor behind her.

"Why, I've been too busy."

"Yeah, snoozing in this recliner."

"And watching the birds," with wide-eyed righteousness, like she was fulfilling her duty. Waiting my turn, I glanced at the busy sparrows on her balcony garden, fluttering and bowing at each other. High above, seabirds caught drafts of the storm clouds. Sunset was firing up over the water beyond the trees.

"There. How d'ya like them apples?"

"Janet Shoemaker, did you cheat?"

"Now, would I do that?" she pouted with droll, innocent baby blues.

"Well, that's one game for you. But don't get cocky; I'm warmed up and ready to start playing now." While we set up for the next game, putting our pieces in tidy rows, reaching past each other's hand to set up the other guy's pieces, like two pushy busybodies, that is, like mother, like daughter. I asked, "Did you hear about the two old ladies sitting in the lobby?"

She smiled expectantly.

"One asks her neighbor, 'Now what was your name again?' The other replies, 'Do you need to know right away?'"

Janet laughed, but then added, "You know, the girls at dinner told me one about those same two old ladies sitting in the lobby. A dapper gentleman approaches them with a polite "good evening," saying that today's his birthday. One lady says to him, 'Well, happy birthday. I'll bet I can guess your exact age.' 'A hundred dollars says you can't.' They all join the bet. Then she says, 'OK, now take off all your clothes.' He doesn't hesitate; it's a warm evening. Both women lean forward and study him head to toe and back again, pausing midway for long, long moments. Finally, nodding and conferring with each other, one of the ladies gives him the verdict: 'You are 93 years old.' Astonished, as he gathers up his clothes to find his wallet, he asks, 'Now, HOW could you tell I turned 93?' 'Oh, you told us yesterday.'"

We both "whooped and hollered," as Mom would say.

"Let's see now," Jazzbo inquired coyly, "Who starts?" Being the winner, she started the next game; she was feigning ignorance to rub it in. I giggled at her lousy sportsmanship. She shrugged modestly; shook her dice cup.

"You know, at our dinner table we have a bet on which waitress is pregnant." She threw and counted by silently nodding her head towards each space, to figure her next move.

"Honestly, Jazzbo," I disapproved. "Say, where did you get your nickname?

"Your Daddy called me 'Jazzbo' when he first saw me dancing in a street parade during high school. I was a flapper then, and everybody started calling me that, even though Janet's a pretty name. Gosh, 75 years I've been Jazzbo."

Now, instead of dancing, she was falling occasionally, becoming more frail. Although slower and mellower, my playful, salty mother was still Jazzbo to me.

"I guess Thad disapproves when I call you 'Jazzbo'. But I like to annoy him. Besides, you ARE Jazzbo, like no one around here knows."

People respected Thad, a bald redheaded guy with large freckles, short and tough. Thad was a retired L.A. fire chief, and nobody could push him around, even at 92. Except Janet. His apartment was, coincidently, directly above hers, so they could holler in the summertime from their balconies. Before they met, his rolled-up sunshade cord would hang down, interfering with her ocean view, so she brazenly cut it off. Later, I tattled; and she shrugged as if she knew nothing of it. She was ever shameless!

"You know," she confided, "Thad eats the same thing every night after dinner: vanilla ice cream with a little chocolate sauce; it never varies. I tempt him to try new things. He won't. He refuses to learn backgammon. He's a stubborn man."

"He sure is good to you."

"I love him to pieces. But when Thad tells me to jump, I say 'How high?' then I do what I want." She smiled impishly.

"One more game," I pointed to her antique 'kitchen' clock, "then time to dress for dinner." Her little ritual: get gorgeous in Auntie Marian's classy castoffs, dangly gold earrings, elegant perfume; make her entrance downstairs, to meet Thad for a hand-hold before the doors are opened to the dining hall.

"Have you noticed how all heads turn when you walk through? Janet, you haven't worn the same outfit twice this year, amazing color combinations, with a smile that lights up the room. I've watched them. When you go past they lean to each other and whisper, their eyes darting at you."

She grinned and set up the next game, while I gasped for air on the balcony. I dipped water, clanking an aluminum measuring cup into Grandma's old galvanized bucket, onto the potted ivy, azaleas, and geraniums. Traipsing through to her bathtub, while I refilled the bucket, I admired how Jazzbo had disguised an institutional bathroom into a romantic event. Soft light from the dusky little counter lamp with 'dingle-dangles,' starched white embroidered eyelet shower curtain, oil portrait of a girl on the wall, rose decal on the toilet lid, and the wine and roses Persian carpet.

I hauled and emptied the bucket onto the rubber tree and ferns on her balcony, while pondering my mother's wellbeing. Her griefs were grieved; she'd made her own arrangements for cremation; her assets were simplified; her belongings fit in one room; she laughed plenty. And she had evenings to cuddle with Thad, whose bathroom lamp matched hers.

"Shut the door, I'm chipping my teeth in here."

I obediently stepped inside and shut her sliding glass door to preserve her stifling heat. I straddled her knees and sat and tossed my dice.

"The other day," Janet confessed, "I made your caramel treat, boiling a can of Eagle brand condensed milk." She raised her eyebrows, "Are you enjoying it?"

I glanced around. There was none. She cackled, "It exploded all over the kitchen ceiling!"

"Woo!" A familiar story. She loved recounting mishaps. "Growing old doesn't cure you, does it? You still do dumb things." I heckled, "Remember when I was a teenager reading a magazine on the sofa, and you watered the living room?" She shot me a withering glance.

My black safely leapt her blockade of whites. She scowled at that. Her big violet eyes, round cheeks, full lips exaggerate her affect—like a cartoon character.

"Anyway," she came to her point: "Thad got up on a ladder to help me clean the goop off the popcorn ceiling. And he scared me, unsteady old man up there. I finally understood what you girls have been saying. I sure won't get on a ladder any more. "

"Oh, yeah? I notice those little birdie figurines up on the curtain valance have shifted places. Didn't you climb up on the ladder to them?"

She shook her silvery head, rattled and threw her dice, saying nothing.

"I know. You just climbed up on the dresser."

She nodded, biting the corner of her mouth.

"And you steadied yourself with your hand on the window?!"

Silence prevailed as she counted out, with slight nods of her head, the possible moves she could make. I helplessly shelved my useless dismay, and proceeded to beat the pants off her.

She took a potty break, I got us some juice and chips, and we set up for the last game. As a magnanimous gesture, Jazzbo offered, "I guess I'll let YOU start this time." I gathered my dice, then halted, mid-throw, and laughed aloud. Her offhanded delivery was droll; I was supposed to start because I had won the last round.

This last game was a long, bloody duel, with cussing, bragging and groaning. She knocked my men off, I built a barricade, which hers jumped anyway; then we knocked each other off so that the game nearly started over. In those days I didn't have to play poorly to give her an edge. Losing was easier then. Losing to Janet at backgammon and monitoring her pills were my only two contributions to my mother's happiness. As a child, I seldom had the power to please her; it was a thrill to be able to do so now.

She counted her last piece off the board, winning again.

"Jazzbo!" I whined.

"Now. Who would YOU say, is the best player (a statement)." I giggled with pleasure; no one gloated more charmingly. Her big blue eyes feigning humility, she was indescribably cute.

I smooched her, replaced my chair, grabbed my purse and the bananas she had swiped for me. I left her to prepare for her 'date,' grateful that Thad's attention kept her much happier than I ever could.

Every evening after supper, they would sit in her place together, and swap stories from their long lives. In the two years they were together, they must have reviewed every detail; this process, once accomplished, enables a person to let go of it all.

One morning Thad didn't wake up.

The management called Janet first, and let her sit by his bed, alone, for a while. After a decent interval, she crept out, smuggling in her bag his matching dusky bathroom lamp with 'dingle-dangles.'

The only grief counseling I provided my mother, across the backgammon board, was to admire how deftly Thad got out of here, and admonish us both to take heed and try to emulate that. She concurred.

Jazzbo didn't find company as good as Thad's; but she didn't have long to grieve, because men were waiting in line. They competed for her with chocolates, expensive perfumes, and soppy cards, entertaining her for a couple more years. She outlived three boyfriends, until finally her sparkle dimmed, along with her hearing and her appetite. So, I appealed to Gladys, who gallantly invited Janet to breakfast with her. For another year, Janet ate one good meal a day. Then Gladys moved away. Janet requested to eat at a little table by herself, and left her food on her plate. That was our first clue she was through.

Then she began to give away the clothes in her closet. She dismissed the antique clocks, sent my sister Nancy scrambling, packing and storing—finally even the hulking grandfather clock was banished.

I entered through her unlocked door, peered down her hallway to her chair, where she was asleep upright on her recliner, uncovered in her nightie, head fallen forward with mouth gaping like a cadaver. Was it a cadaver? No wonder her grandson, Frank, was afraid to visit. I called to her repeatedly, then stood over her and waited for her chest to rise and fall.

"Jazzbo," I gently lifted her head, "why don't you climb into bed and get cozy? You shouldn't sleep like this; you'll get a kink in your neck. And you need to keep your swollen legs up."

She roused slowly. I attached her to her 'Cadillac' walker, and watched her sway towards the bathroom in her bare feet. Her gray hair was flattened in back and radiating from a bald circle, out to the sides.

Pity wrenched my heart as I opened the sliding glass door, sucked in fresh air, to reconnoiter. I noticed no birds bothered to come; there were only husks in their seed dish, plants withering on the balcony, and a messy white sunscreen, shredding and ignored. My mother's bones hurt, all appetite had left, bowel embarrassments kept her home. She was not sick; she was simply 94, and courageous, and dwindling.

After twenty minutes, I awakened her on the toilet, a wad of paper forgotten in her hand. While she roused, I checked her pill boxes into which I had been clicking her medicines, successfully, for seven years. Her morning meds were untouched, and this was late afternoon. I sighed, "Rise and shine, Jazzbo. Stand up."

She could barely hoist her legs into the bed. She moaned with relief when I put her heated hand-warmer, a green beanbag—Nancy's best discovery—under the covers. But my mother's glorious smile looked like a grimace.

I needed to reassess her lifestyle. If discovered in bed all the time, she would be evicted from this facility, but where would she go? To buy more time, I phoned the front desk and lied again to management.

"This is Janet Shoemaker's daughter. I brought some tempting takeout, and we'll eat in the room together, so she won't be down for dinner."

I opened a can of chili, read a whodunit, bedded down on the trundle and watched her sleep around the clock, in her clock-less house. For days, she awoke only for the occasional nap on the toilet. Actually it had been many weeks now that three of us were in relay, taking turns keeping her off the floor, cleaning her up and running interference for her downstairs.

Then my friend Nickie called to say she had a room available in her assisted living facility, and I discussed it with my sister. Nancy came up and we moved Mom with a single suitcase to Nickie's place in Ojai, leaving the Ventura apartment intact.

Nickie was a genius caregiver. It was her passionate calling. She loved and smooched her residents, spoke clearly, and read their minds. After four days Janet had eaten enough of Nickie's food to rally a bit. She hugged me, and asked when Nancy was coming back. I reminded her that as soon as Nancy had healed from a minor surgery, she would come discuss the options, and help Mom decide where she'd best be living.

"I kinda like it here," Janet offered sweetly.

That's how good Nickie was. That was how game Janet was.

So her daughters dismantled her Ventura studio; took time to sit on her littered floor and sort and grieve a bit. And we moved her stuff to Ojai.

I strolled twelve minutes from my place, through a residential neighborhood, to arrive at Nickie's white picket fence. You could tell it was more than a family home only because of potted plastic flowers and the tacky pennants pegged into the lawn that read "People love to come to our house." I entered the front door to see Janet's back to me, amidst a dozen old folks eating silently around three large tables. They seemed to ignore the din of a giant TV screen in the room beyond them, of the dishwasher in the kitchen, of the baby crying and banging his plastic cup on his highchair tray, of Nickie's other children talking with dad in the office, and of women asking if people wanted dessert.

"Hello, folks," I sang out.

"Hello there, Susie," greeted Joe Potts, a client from years back. I waved and smiled.

"Hi, Jazzbo." I kissed my mother from behind her chair.

"Hello, Sweetie." She sipped soup and took a bite of toast. Eating! The mute woman on her right with long straggly gray hair glowered; the woman on her left muttered through missing teeth, wolfing food; but the Potts, across from Jazzbo, were good company. All the women adored Joe's gallantry and ignored his wife. Jazzbo had been here two months, and wouldn't miss a meal once assured that "Potts" was seated in his place.

She was packing away more nourishment than she had in a year. My heart sank. If she rekindled interest in style and decoration, she would not be happy here. She would be cruelly critical of the cluttered, mismatched décor and its unsightly residents.

Imagine that! Her own daughter was miffed because Janet was no longer dying.

Her tiny room, only three times the size of her bed, gratified me as I straightened her pretty flowered sheets. All hers with her marble-topped table, her dresser, her recliner, the starched white eyelet shower curtain over her window and the pretty little oval photos of our grandmothers at age 16, each in her own gold frame. I revered this refuge for my mother as a gift from God.

I hid her potty chair behind her open door; folded Janet's green beanbag on its plate; headed for the kitchen to heat it in the microwave. Passing her table, I noticed that her angry, long-haired companion was throwing a wild-armed, grunting tantrum. From the kitchen, I overheard Jazzbo scold, "Just quiet down, you old crow!" It worked. The woman eyed her with respect and resumed eating. The staff halted like statues, round-eyed. The Potts studied their plates and stifled grins. Content, Jazzbo finished her dinner, then inched her wheeled walker to her room. There I waited with, "You know, that 'old crow' is probably a decade younger than you." Jazzbo dismissed that with a wave of her hand and a glimmer in her eye. She wore matching lavender sweats; the top she had hand-embroidered with purple and blue yarn. She stood with her hands on the black rubber handles of her walker, watching me putter.

"I love your little place here." I refilled her basket of candies, which she kept to bribe her helpers. I searched out hangers in her closet to hang some things draped on her recliner.

"You know, this room is too full. I don't need any of this stuff. I just don't need it." She complained, "and so many clothes in the closet."

"Mom, tell Nantz. I only packed sweats and nighties when you came. When we cleaned out your apartment, Nancy kept picking out more pretty sweaters and slacks sets, and matching shoes. If you don't want them, you need to tell Nancy."

She drove the walker to the bathroom across the hall, while I straightened her bed. When she returned for a nap, I embraced her and kissed her sunken cheek. We were standing there when she announced,

"I wish I would just DIE."

"Jazzbo," I put my face right in hers. "You WERE dying. Then you started EATING again. Get a grip!" I chastised.

"Now, is it my turn?" Janet had frequent tiny spells and forgot where she was in her game.

"Yup, your turn." It wasn't. But if she got more moves, it helped level the playing field, now that she was so foggy.

Wincing, she pried open her cramping 'trigger-fingers' before moving her pieces on the board, counting aloud.

"Well, now, how do you like them apples?" She had miscounted in her favor.

"I'll getcha. Don't get smug." I tossed and moved. Then I waited for her to deliberate, stare off, then refocus and deliberate again, giving me time to observe that she was fading, that we had made the right decision and she belonged here. My mother was 'dwindling,' as we hospice workers used to say.

"Now, did I move for this dice?" The game was distressing her.

"I don't think you moved at all." A lie.

"Oh, I can't think straight." Her lips curved down in the grimace which heralded tears.

"Are you tired, Mrs. S.?" I sat next to her with my arm around her and she laid her head on my shoulder, cuddling in, letting me hold her a while as Shoey might have. I asked, "Want to quit?"

"I think so."

I snapped the backgammon case closed, knowing it was for the last time. I removed it from the seat of her walker, on which I placed two tiny glasses, and some shortbread on a Kleenex.

"How about a treat?"

"Bailey's Irish Cream," she lit up. She stayed seated on the edge of her bed, wide-eyed as a child; and I shut her door to dig out of her closet the only thing she still relished. I returned to my cushion on the bedside commode. The cocoa brown liquor oozed out of the bottle and plumped soundlessly into our glasses.

"Cheers," we clinked and sipped. She smacked her lips, giving her head one quick sideways toss of approval with wink, tuck of cheek, cluck of tongue.

"Man, that's laripin'." She remembered Daddy's old phrase.

"Mmm? mm!" I agreed. We nibbled cookie. "I remember when you'd give Daddy an order, without any 'please,' and patiently, he'd say, 'Yes, Dove.'"

She didn't reply; just more sipping, and vacuuming out the dregs, and licking her lips. I rejoiced in her well-being as I walked home. Her life was closing down naturally, without suffering. In fact, during the days that my mother dwindled, I was elated for her.

After an innocuous fall off her bed, at age 94, Janet Shoemaker was sent to E.R., where they did every blood test and exam and x-ray possible. She got a thorough workup with a full bill of health, and was sent home with four days of pills for a minor urinary tract infection.

Back at Nickie's, she dressed for breakfast every morning;

then stayed in bed the rest of the day. They would deliver something to her room, or sometimes sit and spoon-feed her.

One of those days, I visited to find her asleep, prone on her bed, with a sandwich plate sitting on her middle, her tiny hand lying across a slim peanut butter and jelly sandwich, as if she had dozed off mid-intention. Teasing her as usual, I woke her with, "Janet. WHERE is your sandwich?"

"Oh," she muttered, eyes still closed, "Half was enough."

"But Jazzbo, your hand is resting on the WHOLE sandwich—two perfect white triangles." Without moving her hand or opening her eyes, she considered that.

Finally, she spoke.

"I think I'm just going to waste away."

A week later, her two daughters crossed the empty hospital waiting room and sat in a corner, seeking privacy to speak their minds.

"Nancy, did you notice? The doc didn't say 'I'm giving her IV antibiotics for the sepsis of the blood.' He said, 'Do you want me to?' There's choice here. Does he treat her, or let her die quickly and easily?"

Nancy looked me in the eye and said, "You're 'done', aren't you, Susie?" Her directness surprised me.

So did my "Yes." I heard myself tell her that I'd been 'done' since before we moved her to Ojai. "But you're not, are you?"

"I just don't want her to suffer," Nancy hedged. "Urinary tract infection hurts her."

"But she always immediately alerted the doc; this time she didn't even notice. And it's gone to her blood. Nancy, SHE is 'done.'"

"I don't see that. We've never talked about it."

"Dr. Nelson's same choice with his own dad tells us she won't suffer, because he wouldn't have let his father suffer."

"I don't know, I've seen her close to death so many times, and with my care she rallied."

"That's true. But maybe she rallied for YOU? She's two

different people: Your Jazzbo likes pretty new things and surprises that you bring her; my Jazzbo is tired of this life, watching herself lose her edge in backgammon, wishing she could slip away. She's beyond pretty things. She can't hear people, yet refuses her hearing aids; avoids looking or reading in spite of 20/15 vision; she's bored and tired of bone pain. Now we find a bed sore; more will come, because she is not eating or exercising. Broken and painful; her little old body is dissolving away, as we speak. Let's not imply she should dwell in it any longer. She has been signaling that she's done, for a year now. You need to ask her, talk with her about it. Have you?"

"No."

"Then you need more time. You and I have different paces, and I've seen dying people time their exit according to the slowest one in the family. So you call the shots. I have her durable power-of-attorney for health care, but I am following your lead now. It's between you and her; it's up to you two, no one else."

"Don't make ME decide."

"Nancy, I've made my decision. No more antibiotics. That's what I would want for me, and I think the golden rule works here. But she gets antibiotics until YOU are ready, that's all."

She fiddled with her hair, her beautifully hooded amber eyes stricken. But she gamely deliberated, while I added, "The IV fluids she is getting here brighten her up and will buy you a few good days with her, back at Nickie's."

I left my sister in the lobby and returned to the nurses' station. A few minutes later she joined me, just as I was requesting further medicine from the nurse.

"No," Nancy stopped us. "No more antibiotics. Some survive without them; let's leave it up to her. 'Let go and let God'."

"OK, Nantz."

Luckily, the hospital was full, so our mother was given a bed in the intensive care unit —a private room, perfect for a meeting. The fancy air-in-sand bed weighed her in at 97 pounds: two thirds of her normal weight. Monitors and machinery behind her were all silent; their counter light shone on her silver hair. She was at ease, and, thanks to the fluids she was receiving through her wrist, lucid between snoozes. We gathered around her bed, her two daughters, her compassionate doctor, and a

Hospice nurse. This was every hospice counselor's dream-come-true: fully open communication, and everyone in accord.

Janet opened her eyes to see that she was the center of attention and she milked it.

I resumed my old role of facilitating, "Well, Dr. Nelson, this is Janet Shoemaker, your new patient. You are her grandson, Frank's, doctor. This is no emergency; Janet is just here to get a physician's order for hospice."

"Yes, I've been too busy in ER to get to her, so I had her admitted for the night."

"Janet," I shouted near her ear, "this is your doctor, Dr. Nelson; you finally get to meet him."

"Hello, Mrs. Shoemaker, we're going to keep you comfortable. How are you feeling now?"

"Oh, just fine. Now. Tell me your name."

"Doug Nelson."

"Doug Nelson," she repeated with the sparkling smile of old, and blinking her eyes at him with squeezes, like little hugs.

"And this is your hospice nurse," I continued, "who will visit you at Nickie's house, back in your own bed. Her name is Carol and she and I have worked together for many years. Carol will take good care of you."

"Hello, Mrs. Shoemaker."

"Would you hold my hand?" It was Janet's pouting voice.

"Sure I will," Carol said, and laughed as she approached the bedside and took our mother's hand. They grinned at each other over their knotted hands, as if posing for an ad about a friendly vacation package.

Nancy and I stood back while Jazzbo gathered her crew around her, sweetly and willingly welcoming in the end of her lifetime.

Nickie's integrity was intact. Janet never was required to go the dining room, never forced to eat; yet when willing, was always fed. Nickie spoiled her, knowing that Jazzbo ate up the loving attention served with the ice cream.

In bed, because of the wound at her tailbone, she mostly faced the wall. So I hung her best picture of young Shoey just at her eye level.

"Now isn't that nice," she said so gently when she peered

at it.

"Have you seen him lately?" I asked her.

She said nothing, kept looking at Shoey's photo, at his arresting heavy-lidded dark eyes in deep sockets, and sensual, rounded perfect lips, dark hair, dressed in his tie and dress suit with one arm akimbo, a shy smile....

A few days later, while spooning softened ice cream into Janet's willing little beak, Nickie asked innocently,

"Who's that?"

"Shoey"

"Who is Shoey?"

"My husband, the girls' father. We met in high school 80 years ago."

"How do you spell that name?"

"S.h.o.e.y." His name was Orin Henderson Shoemaker, after his father. But everyone called him "Shoey."

She had not mentioned him much lately. Was it Nickie's interest, or maybe he was hovering? Reassuring her? Would Jazzbo be joining him soon?

When Nancy came, those weekends in February, she stayed day and night with Mom, sometimes dozing in her recliner next to the bed, sometimes chatting with the night girl, helping set tables for breakfast.

My sister's phone call awoke me from a deep sleep.

"Hi, Sooz."

"What time is it?"

"4:10. I don't think she's breathing, Sooz."

"Oh." Stupefied, I stood at the phone, shivering in the dark.

"I left her room for a few minutes, and when I came back, she was just the same, except not breathing," Nancy explained.

"She did it. Good for her. Most people slip away once they're alone, even if it's only for a moment."

"I haven't told anybody yet, thinking you'd like to come sit silently with her a moment, before all the commotion starts."

"Thanks, Nantz, I'll be right over."

I prayed by her bed. I noticed that her waxen face resembled any other peacefully dead face, mouth ajar, eyes closed in sleep. Except for her nose. Janet had an unusual profile, one I've never seen anywhere else, except in a Dutch portrait, a nice nose that blended with her gorgeous face, the beauty being in the slight imperfection, and the charm of person. Charm gone. Beauty gone. Just Mommy's nose still there.

As I sat, I imagined that Daddy came to usher her over. And that they were already dancing, young and happy and nicely dressed, dancing close and smooth the Balboa, a clipped foxtrot with tiny speedy steps and quick little toe embellishments, one figure with four legs interlaced, in perfect happy rhythm.

Then I pictured what it was like being warm and safe in the soft wet organ-pillows of her womb, gently rocked as she danced. Bopping around in her cushy womb while she was happy, the center of attention, the belle of the ball, with the man who loved her, tripping along that Dixie rhythm.

Over a thousand dolphins set the sea to boiling once again, swimming along with us as we headed out to Channel Islands on the tour boat, ostensibly to spy gray whales migrating north.

We five were smuggling Janet's ashes in new little white paper bags in our windbreaker pockets. We had skulked onto the touring boat, uneasy about strewing without the captain's permission. That was on purpose. Janet loved stolen fruit, and this 'steal' of $125 for a whale watch instead of $1000 for a funeral boat, would 'tickle her silly.'

Cousin Alan, the seaworthy one, chose the back bench looking back to shore, where we parked our stuff; told us to keep our eyes on the horizon of land we'd just left, until our stomachs accommodated to the motion of the boat. And we chewed candied ginger.

Each of us delighted at the multitude of sleek creatures frisking effortlessly alongside our speeding boat, surfacing so prettily, zooming through the hazel water. After the pod of dolphins pulled away from us, the trip was uneventful, not a gray whale in sight. The skipper kept the humans up front on two decks, distracted with ogling a couple of lazy humpback whales. Our family of five discreetly drifted back to regroup at our seats. We huddled at the back railing, level with the rolling water, inhaling the salty air and exhaust fumes.

Without a word, we strewed Janet's ashes into the wake of our boat; dropped the white bags in and watched them bob and recede into the rushing water. Daddy's ashes were waiting out there along this coast where both folks had grown up and lived their lives.

Frank and I touched heads and chanted an ancient prayer, our voices muted by the knocking of the engines. But the prayer folded into the slapping waters with her ashes, lofted into the chilly air with her fresh spirit. We all five hugged, shed a tear or two for the flux of all life, including our own. We sang two vintage songs, popular when Jazzbo and Shoey were courting, their love-songs, which Mommy had sung to us as kids:

"Button up your overcoat when the wind blows free. Take good care of yourself; you belong to me."

"...when we're dancing, I don't know why, I love you like I do. I don't know why, I just do."

Dear Reader,

You are simply a human being. Once you have read all this material and done your "house" cleaning, then set this book aside.

Release your own apprehensions. Tap that natural humility, that sense of worth, that peace, and that love which is your essence. And go stand by your neighbor in distress. You can do it. Easy. Just be your quietest self.

We all have our small chance at life and its sweetness. We all hurt. We all die. And we all need each other.

Blessings upon us.

Love, Susie

Affairs in Order?

1. Second signature on checking account, and/or power of attorney.
2. Index of Vital Information—on self, dependents, pets. (See Appendix 2)
3. Disposition and funeral preferences expressed.
4. Durable power of attorney for health care.
5. Will, and/or living trust, and/or T.O.D. and/or property titles transferred, etc.
6. Assets listed, clarified—taught to survivors.
7. Verbal permission, apology, gratitude, and forgiveness, while of sound mind NOW, to next generation, for when you can no longer live alone THEN, and will need their supervision.
8. Learn how to receive, to relinquish control/power.
9. Cherished belongings listed or labeled.
10. Procedure and prices for selling cars, jewelry, extra vehicles.
11. Dump obsolete possessions. Clean out that garage or closet, and make a legible, correct address book.
12. Confidential papers/diaries/photos censored and/or destroyed.
13. Family photos sorted, labeled and dispersed.
14. Reduce dwelling to fit your needs and abilities.
15. Keep home repaired—towards sale or widowhood.
16. Teach spouse, or write instructions for, your household jobs: finances, computer, laundry, cooking, and maintenance of the yard, orchard, animals, vehicles.
17. Instructions for running or selling the family business.
18. Family video made.
19. Letters/tapes for loved ones to find after you are gone.
20. Make amends, settle disputes, drop animosities and forgive.
21. Relinquish hope for what cannot be—accept yourself as you are!
22. Love now; be kind while you still have the chance.

Index of Vital Info

- Name/Address/Phones/E-Mail/Driver's License #/SS #/DOB
- Autos: license #, model, year, color, VIN #, location of pink slip and registration, insurance co. and policy #, locations of all keys, maintenance records, owner's manual
- Dependents: names, DOB, SS #, nicknames, teachers, social worker, MD's, alternate caretakers, etc.
- Pets: name, breed, color, age, weight, food, medicine, toilet regimes, alternate caretakers, command words
- Property maintenance: names, phone #, landlord, plumber, gardener
- MDs: name, specialty, phone #, address, appointment frequency
- Broker, Investor, Account #
- Income sources: when, where, how it comes in
- Banking: bank, account type, account #
- Safe deposit box—location of key and bank
- Military records, discharge papers, veterans' benefits
- Clubs/associations/fraternities: contact names and phone numbers.
- Monthly bills to pay (rent, utilities, gym, mortgage, car payment, credit cards)
- Debts—owed to me and by me
- Insurances: where policies filed, claim #, company name, phone #
- Wills/trusts/power of attorney: where filed, attorney's name and phone #
- Legal documents—where to find certificates: (deeds, patents, copyrights, birth, death, guardianship, conservatorship, marriage, divorce, adoption, passport)
- Funeral preferences, mortuary address and phone #
- List of all acquaintances to be notified at your death
- Valuables: history, value, where located, alternate guardian
- Computer codes, e-mail addresses, etc.

Medical Decisions

Your doctor must tell you about your medical condition and what different treatments can do for you. Many treatments have side effects. Your doctor must offer you information about serious problems that medical treatment is likely to cause you. Often, more than one treatment might help you—and people have different ideas about which is best. Your doctor can tell you which treatments are available to you, but s/he cannot choose for you.

When your doctor gives you information and advice about medical treatment, you have the right to choose. You can say 'Yes' to treatments you want. You can say 'No' to treatments you don't want—even if the treatment might keep you alive longer.

If you cannot make treatment decisions, your doctor will ask your closest available relative or friend to help decide what is best for you. Most of the time, that works. But sometimes everyone doesn't agree about what to do. That's why it is helpful if you say in advance what you want to happen if you can't speak for yourself. There are several kinds of 'advance directives' that you can use to say what you want and who you want to speak for you.

One kind of advance directive under California law lets you name someone to make health care decisions when you can't. This document is called the DURABLE POWER OF ATTORNEY FOR HEALTH CARE.

You can fill out this form if you are 18 years or older and of sound mind. You do not need a lawyer to fill it out; you only need your signature notarized.

You can choose an adult relative or friend you trust as your 'agent' to speak for you whenever you become too sick or impaired to make your own decisions.

You discuss what you want done with that person. You write down in the DURABLE POWER OF ATTORNEY FOR HEALTH CARE when you would or would not want medical treatment. In the 'optional' space you list specific life-prolonging and comfort treatments you would or would not want (see Appendix 4).

Talk to your doctor about what you want and give your doctor a copy of the document. Give another copy to the person named as your agent. And take a copy with you when you travel or go into a hospital or other treatment facility.

Sometimes treatment decisions are hard to make and it truly helps your family and your doctors if they know what you prefer. THE DURABLE POWER OF ATTORNEY FOR HEALTH CARE also gives them legal protection when they follow your wishes.

If you do not have anybody to make decisions for you, you can use another kind of advance directive to write down your wishes about treatment. This is often called a 'living will' because it takes effect while you are still alive but have become unable to speak for yourself. The California Natural Death Act lets you sign a living will called a DECLARATION. Anyone 18 years or older and of sound mind can sign one.

A signed declaration tells your doctor directly (without the intervening agent—the friend or relative) that you don't want any treatment that would only prolong your dying. All life-sustaining treatment would be stopped if you were terminally ill and your death was expected soon, or if you were permanently unconscious. You would still receive treatment to keep you comfortable, however.

The doctor must follow your wishes about limiting treatment or turn your care over to another doctor who will. Your doctors are also legally protected when they follow your wishes.

SUMMARY OF DOCUMENTS

You can change or revoke any of these documents at any time as long as you can communicate your wishes:

• A DURABLE POWER OF ATTORNEY FOR HEALTH CARE lets you name someone to make treatment decisions for you. That person can make most medical decisions, not just those about life-sustaining treatment, when you can't speak for yourself. Besides naming an agent, you can also use the form to say when you would and wouldn't want particular kinds of treatment. This is your ADVANCE DIRECTIVE.

- If you don't want to name someone to make decisions when you can't, you can request directly of your doctor by signing the NATURAL DEATH ACT DECLARATION. This DECLARATION says that you do not want life-prolonging treatment if you are terminally ill or permanently unconscious.

- A DNR (DO NOT RESUSCITATE) form, signed by your physician, is the only document paramedics in California may obey, and only if it has their California EMSA logo on it. EMT paramedics are mandated to do full life support whenever they are called out with 911, no matter whether the other above documents are in place or not. But in a crisis, if they are called and shown this DNR form signed by the physician, they are allowed to provide comfort measures only (CMO), and not do full CPR (cardiopulmonary resuscitation) on a patient. This document is mainly appropriate for the extremely elderly or for those already ill or severely damaged—in other words, for those already approaching death before the crisis occurred.

Local hospitals provide basic forms, for free, and will require them at intake—so you may as well get yours ready before they are required. As new forms come out, you will need to address them too, but now you will be prepared for them.

Specific Instructions

SPECIFIC INSTRUCTIONS are suggested here that you might consider writing in your advance directive documents:

If I am incurably ill or damaged or actively dying...

- The following comfort measures I DO WANT, as I consider them not significantly prolonging the dying process:

or

- The following measures I DO NOT WANT, as I consider them unnecessarily prolonging the dying process:

or

- I WANT the following comfort/life support measures to be administered AS LONG AS they increase my comfort, and do not significantly prolong the dying process:

or

- I wish for all comfort/life-support measures to be administered to ensure every possible opportunity for me to sustain life.

- Treatments to consider allowing or refusing in the above statements:
    - Morphine or other pain-control (possibly addictive) drugs
    - IV fluids
    - Tube feedings
    - Antibiotics (treatment for tangential infection, pneumonia or flu, or bladder infection)
    - Oxygen
    - Respirator
    - Cardiopulmonary resuscitation
    - Surgery for unrelated issues, which will not reverse the dying process (i.e. open-heart surgery for a cancer patient, amputating an infected limb)

- Chemotherapy or radiation treatment as curative measures
- Radiation only for pain control
- Dialysis
- Heart medications
- Insulin
- Etc.

To get more current information about advance directives, ask your lawyer, doctor, nurse, social worker, hospital admitting desk, or public health department.

Funeral Arrangements

In your meeting at the funeral home you will cover items such as:

Social Security benefits, obituaries, obtaining certified copies of the death certificate, veteran's benefits, setting times for viewing and burial or cremation, contacting clergy or officiate for a service. Set times for services or visitation only AFTER confirming with funeral home.

Bring what you need to make arrangements at the funeral home:

* A list of any questions, requests, or concerns you might have.
* Burial clothes and recent photo (if you want burial or viewing)
* Veteran's discharge papers (for veteran benefits or a military funeral)
* Cemetery deed or any other burial information already in place
* Information needed by funeral director for death certificate and obituary (just bring whatever you have):

1. Full name of deceased
2. Date and place of birth
3. Address of last residence; number of years in County
4. Social Security number
5. Military service: branch, years of service, honors
6. Marital status; date(s) of marriage(s) & name of spouse(s)
7. Education: years completed, degrees awarded, honors
8. Occupation(s)
9. Place of employment; kind of business; number of years employed
10. Children—names & birth dates
11. Children by previous marriages
12. Father's full name and state or country of birth
13. Mother's full name, maiden name, state or country of birth
14. Location of final resting place
15. Date of death, place and cause
16. Name of organizations with membership and/or offices held
17. List of honors or accomplishments

How many official copies of the death certificate will you need? Consider the following needs for a death certificate:

- To collect proceeds of a life insurance policy. If there is more than one policy with separate companies, each company will need one.
- To transfer ownership or title of anything with the deceased's name on the title. This includes real estate (one for each piece of property), bank and brokerage accounts, stocks & bonds, automobiles, boats, mobile homes.
- Social Security does NOT need one—the funeral director notifies this agency.
- Some banks, savings and loans, and the DMV will give the certificate back (making themselves a copy), so it can be used again.

Family Records and Info

Following is a list of items experts say should be available in every family in the event of death. Not all items apply to all families. In many cases, information should be included for both husband and wife. Every individual could write his/her own brief obituary so that it may be immediately available.

IMMEDIATE REQUIREMENTS

1. Date of birth
2. Place of birth
3. Social Security number
4. Mortuary preference
5. Notify clergy
6. Notify immediate family
7. Notify family doctor (date, time, cause, of death)
8. Name/address of any company having funeral contract
9. Other funeral info, i.e. grave deed

PEOPLE TO NOTIFY

1. Family and relatives
2. Doctor
3. Clergy
4. Attorney
5. Close friends
6. Employer/Employees
7. Neighbors
8. Insurance agent
9. Lodges, fraternities, clubs
10. DMV
11. Social Security

IMPORTANT RECORDS TO HAVE ON HAND:

- Social Security Card
- Birth Certificate
- Last Will & Testament - locations of original and copies
- I.R.S. Form #706
- Bank account records/checkbook
- Savings account passbook
- Investments, CD's, IRA's
- Keys—house, car, office, etc.
- Marriage license
- Driver's license
- Employment record
- Automobile registration
- Mortgages & trust deeds
- Credit cards/charge accounts
- Diplomas/degrees
- Safe deposit box location and key
- Insurance policies/Life, Health, Group
- Patent papers/copyrights
- Deeds to real estate
- Record of business ventures
- List of people who owe money to you
- List of outstanding debts
- Income tax returns from previous year
- Name of stock broker/location of securities
- Employment benefits/profit sharing, pension, stock options, termination dates
- Liabilities/record of debts and contract payments
- Military records/Discharge paper and veteran's benefits
- Computer access codes, e-mail addresses

CATALOG POSSESSIONS

- Personal property, clothes, jewelry, etc.
- Real estate
- Automobiles, other vehicles
- Furniture and appliances
- Collections
- Keepsakes, antiques
- Hidden assets
- Other valuables

Memorial of Me

MEMORIAL OF ME (helpful info to have in your Vital Info file):

- I would like the following (religious) (spiritual) (philosophical) convictions expressed at my funeral:
- I would like to leave the following messages:
- Some of my accomplishments that I feel good about are:
- One of my fondest memories is:
- My favorite scripture – quote – poem:
- One of the greatest inspirations in my life has been:
- If I could live my life again, I would:
- The place on this earth that I have enjoyed the most is:
- One of the greatest pleasures I have enjoyed has been:
- The activities I have enjoyed the most have been:
- The kind of music that I have enjoyed most is:
- My favorite story is:
- My favorite flower is:
- My favorite color is:
- I am most grateful for:
- I want to say goodbye to: _____ (in person) (by phone) (by letter) (on tape or video)
- These attitudes and behaviors I want to carry to the grave:
- These are the attitudes and behaviors I observe in myself which I do not want to carry to the grave:
- If I were to develop a different human relations exercise for each member of my family that would be helpful for them to deal with their sense of loss at my death; I would have: _____do_____
- The final thought I would like to leave my family and friends is:
- The last thing I want to do for myself before I die is:
- I would like the following (words) (design) (symbol) on my (tombstone) (headstone) (epitaph):

Alzheimer's, Anyone?

(Author's letter to her family, a personal statement for your consideration)

I'm becoming forgetful in annoying ways. It worries me. If my friends/ family/work colleagues were to insist that I consult with a neurologist and he were to tell me the worst—that most likely I had Alzheimer's—what would I do? Here are my thoughts:

The initial terror and panic would be suffocating. Then my instinct would be to make it a secret, to hide the problem from others. Neither fear nor dissembling is productive. So, to bring things back into perspective, so that I could live with this news in my life, I have thought out: (1) what Alzheimer's means to me, (2) how I see my future now, (3) what I can do about it, and (4) what I can't, my faith.

Alzheimer's is a slow, terminal disease—perhaps not terminal in 7 months, perhaps more like 7 years. My first big losses are: my future, the ability to trust myself, my independence, especially my cherished solitude. My biggest fear is that, before I lose my life, I might lose touch with my beloved Lord, I might forget Him. These are big losses, and I will have to rely upon faith, and maybe drugs when I forget faith, to balm the torment of living in a frayed and tattered mind.

Alzheimer's is a disease of the brain which causes the brain to slowly lose its ability to function. Remember, the brain is not me, not my soul or spirit, not my innate goodness and peace. The brain is not the seat of love. The brain is merely a physical organ which can be diseased just like a heart or a lung or a liver. If I had a fast heart attack, I would not be ashamed and I would tell others and expect sympathy. Now that I am having a slow brain attack, I refuse to be ashamed, and I will probably embarrass myself (so what's new?) but I will tell others and expect kindness and understanding.

The job of the brain is to direct the other organs in keeping the body alive—it is the chief communicating organ of this body. When it deteriorates, it loses its ability to commandeer the body, and little functions go awry— word-finding, memory, cognitive logic and figuring out stuff, whether to use good hygiene at the toilet, whether to use the toilet at all, how to control the excretory muscle system, whether to direct traffic down the esophagus or the trachea—whether to send air into the stomach or saliva and other matter into the lungs. Often lung infection—pneumonia as a direct effect of the brain's dysfunction—is what causes death in Alzheimer's patients. Either that, or the inability to swallow at all, and the resulting lack of food and fluid, causes the death. It is my personal experience that these can be very comfortable, perhaps even euphoric, ways to die.

Death is not the enemy. Extended life with a malfunctioning brain is the enemy. The BIG PROBLEM is: who will look after me until I die? Who will take care of me while allowing me to die as quickly as I can?

I will need someone (or more than one) to stand by me when my own brain no longer tells me what to do. It is likely I will be scared, difficult, acting inappropriately. I will be a paranoiac lost lamb who needs constant companionship, constant protection and restriction, constant guidance, constant reassurance. And most likely I will not remember that I need the person(s) and I will not cooperate with them and I will drive them nuts. So who will remain loyal to a losing me? Especially, who will help me with #6 and #7 below? I do not know. I have faith that you will be here. Whoever you are, I thank you from the bottom of my heart, and I pray that God reward you—that you will be ultimately happy and clothed in grace.

I am very clear about this: I will NOT commit suicide. I am equally clear about this: as my brain dies, SO SHALL MY BODY. As I contract infection due to my own malfunction, I will NOT be treated for that infection. As I forget to eat or drink, or refuse to eat or drink, I shall NOT eat or drink, and death naturally by lack of food or fluid will NOT take seven years, and it will be a relatively comfortable, possibly euphoric, death.

So, between now and then, what do I do? My list:

1. *Grieve. My life, my self-image, as I have known it, is over. I need to wail, weep, piss and moan, rage, release, let it go, honestly and courageously accept that this is the way it is. Big job!*

2. *Finish business. Quit my jobs, gather my eggs in one basket, cash in my chips, finish my projects or pass them on to others, update plans for any disabled relative's well-being and future, adopt out*

animals, check off the items on my own list, "Are Your Affairs in Order?"

3. *Let go of obsolete belongings. Pitch professional wardrobe, camping gear, old files, etc. Sell cars and diamonds. Give valuables to appreciative others, keep only comfortable washable dementia-patient clothes like sweat suits, house coats, T-shirts, elastic-waist slacks, etc.*

4. *Goodbye party. Let's say our goodbyes while we're able to laugh and tattle on each other.*

5. *Find a last dwelling, with view of trees or sea or sunset sky, and good people to keep me clean and comfortable there.*

6. *Refrain from meals—as soon as my brain does not tell me to eat, or as soon as I lose interest in food, or as soon as I can comfortably refrain from food willingly. (A food-free environment would be helpful, since demented people sometimes can copy whatever others are doing, because the social imitative part of the brain often still functions.)*

7. *Prayer time. Devotional music, prayer, sounds of worship always available to my ears. Devotional readings and prayer-beads. Walking under sky, in forests, at water's edge, at dawn and dusk—this is my church. Or sit there when unable to walk. At least a big window to look upon a tree dancing in the wind. And always my little altar with flowers and candlelight.*

8. *Medications. As needed to keep me comfortable, such as antidepressant, anti-anxiety, or allergy pills. No life-prolonging medications or procedures, such as antibiotics, tubal feeding, heart medicine, insulin, dialysis.*

9. *Dwindle nicely. And in timely manner, allowing time for letting go, and yet not outliving myself. Not exhausting my caregivers, yet time enough to thank them. Bless their hearts.*

Dehydration vs. 'Dying of Thirst'

Physicians used to routinely order IV fluids for terminally ill patients to prevent what they believed to be the agony of 'dying of thirst,' and most of us still tend to expect those IVs.

Many nurses, particularly those who work with the dying, have found otherwise—that dehydration is not painful; that dehydration is actually beneficial.

As death approaches, dehydration occurs naturally from inadequate drinking. Transitory thirst, dry mouth, and changes in mental status have been found to develop. The mental changes—while upsetting to relatives—seem to bring relief to patients by lessening their awareness of suffering.

Fluid deprivation eliminates the frequent use of a urinal or bedpan or commode, and the discomfort that goes along with it.

Dehydration relieves lung congestion and the symptoms associated with it. (IV fluids make breathing harder, because when the body is shutting down naturally, it is not prepared to process all that extra fluid.)

Dehydration reduces such painful symptoms as nausea and vomiting, and diminishes the risk of bedsores.

Dry-mouth is dehydration's only drawback, which can be relieved with good care. To ease dry-mouth, offer ice chips and apply lip balm to chapped, dry lips. Avoid lemon and glycerin swabs, as they promote dryness—just clean out the patient's mouth with plain cotton swabs, moistened in plain water.

Accompanied by comfort measures and emotional support, dehydration is a humane, therapeutic way to help dying patients benefit from this natural means of pain relief.

Do confirm this concept with a hospice nurse.

Tasks of Mourning

Being informed of the death,

witnessing the death,

announcing the death,

planning or preparing the service,

attending the service,

strewing the ashes,

ordering the marker,

changing names on legal documents,

disposing of clothes and belongings,

writing to relatives,

writing and re-reading the obituary,

visiting and re-visiting the graveside,

rearranging house to suit the survivors,

going to places you used to attend together, and especially,

talking about your loved one,

telling stories about your life together.

List of Homework Assignments:

1. Visit nursing home. Compare daily cost with hotel prices.
2. Interview in-home employer; ask four questions.
3. Converse with a demented person.
4. Make your own Index of Vital Info (Appendix 2).
5. List retirement homes in your area, and visit one with gift and thanks.
6. List your own Social History facts, add to Vital Info files.
7. Collect own obituary statistics (Appendix 5).
8. Wheelchair ride.
9. Ponder what would you be doing if you had six months left to live.
10. Discuss your end-of-life care if you had dementia.
11. Edit the suggested list for putting affairs in order, to make it your own (Appendix 1).
12. Dialogue with an 18-year-old about donating organs.
13. Start work on your own Affairs in Order list, easiest one first.
14. Discuss your funeral preferences.
15. Recall and discuss your or friend's experience of a 'good death.'
16. Plan your own disposition through the 4 steps (tell it, write it, register it, pay for it).
17. List tasks of mourning you accomplished when bereaved.
18. Consider two simplifications in your holiday customs.
19. Make a list of gratitudes.
20. Have a conversation to practice listening.
21. Locate the closest professional who specializes in bereavement counseling.
22. Plan your own memorial gathering.
23. Use one tip with a bereaved person.
24. Locate nearest volunteer hospice, get acquainted, and add info to Vital Docs.

Made in the USA
Charleston, SC
23 July 2016